Unrelenting Change, Innovation, and Risk

The Association of Community College Trustees and Rowman & Littlefield Publishers: The Futures Series on Community Colleges

Sponsored by the Association of Community College Trustees and Rowman & Littlefield Publishers, *The Futures Series on Community Colleges* is designed to produce and deliver books that strike to the heart of issues that will shape the future of community colleges. Futures books examine emerging structures, systems, and business models, and stretch prevailing assumptions about leadership and management by reaching beyond the limits of convention and tradition.

Topics addressed in the *series* are those that are vital to community colleges, but have yet to receive meaningful attention in literature, research, and analysis. *Futures Series* books are written by scholars and practitioners who deliver a unique perspective on a topic or issue—a president or higher education consultant bringing expert and practical understanding to a topic, a policy analyst breaking down a complex problem into component parts, an academic or think tank scholar conducting incisive research, or a researcher and a practitioner working together to examine an issue through different lenses.

Futures books are developed on the premise that disruptive innovation and industry transformation are, and will be, an ongoing challenge. Gradual improvement is, understandably, a natural preference of leaders. It will not be enough, however, to position our colleges for the future. The future will be about transformation and, to perform optimally, our colleges will need to become capable of large-scale change. As leaders come face-to-face with digital forces and rapidly changing social, economic, and public policy conditions, they will have no choice but to get ahead of change or relinquish market position to competitors. *Futures* books are a vehicle through which leaders can learn about and prepare for what's ahead. Whether it's through analysis of what big data will mean in the next generation of colleges, or which business models will become the new normal, *Futures* books are a resource for practitioners who realize that the ideas of out-of-the-box thinkers and the innovative practices of high-performing organizations can be invaluable for answering big questions and solving complex problems.

Richard L. Alfred, Series Co-editor
Emeritus Professor of Higher Education
University of Michigan

Debbie Sydow, Series Co-editor
President
Richard Bland College of the College of William and Mary

Forthcoming Books in *The Futures Series on Community Colleges*

Developing Tomorrow's Leaders: Context, Challenges, and Capabilities
By Pamela Eddy, Debbie L. Sydow, Richard L. Alfred, and Regina L. Garza Mitchell
This book provides a template for leadership development in the community college sector. The theme of the book focuses on the need to move beyond hierarchical leadership to networked leadership that taps talent throughout the institution. The transformational change required in the two-year sector demands new approaches to leading, including tolerance for risk, use of data analytics, and a focus on relationships. New and alternative means for leadership development are presented

The Urgency of Now: Equity and Excellence
By Marcus M. Kolb, Samuel D. Cargile, et al
The Urgency of Now asserts that in addition to being granted access to the community college, all twenty-first-century students need uncompromised support to succeed. Success means demonstrating relevant learning for transfer and employment, and timely completion of credentials. Looking to the future, the authors contend that community colleges, both by their past successes and future challenges, are at the epicenter for determining the essential ingredients of a new student-centered system that guarantees equity and excellence.

Financing America's Community Colleges: Where We Are, Where We're Going
By Richard Romano and James Palmer
Grounded in an economic perspective, *Financing America's Community Colleges* helps college leaders make sense of the challenges they face in securing and managing the resources needed to carry out the community college mission. Finance has perpetually been an Achilles heel for leaders at all levels of management. With the premise that leaders are better at winning battles they know something about, this book equips leaders with an understanding of the fundamentals and the complexities of community college finance. It tackles current and emerging issues with insight that is analytic and prophetic—a must read for current and prospective leaders.

The Completion Agenda in Community Colleges: What It Is, Why It Matters, and Where It's Going
By Chris Baldwin
Community colleges in many states are facing intensifying pressure from policy-makers for improved student outcomes overtly manifested in aggressive performance-based funding formulas. In this book, Chris Baldwin asks and answers an overarching question: Are community colleges, government agencies, foundations, and other entities aware of the unintended consequences of actions related to the completion agenda? The book explores the potential benefit of increased educational attainment and credentials versus the possible sacrifice of quality and the labor market value of the credentials awarded.

Institutional Analytics: Building a Culture of Evidence
By Karen Stout

Institutional Analytics paints a clear picture of the challenges involved in cultural change and building a team capable of using analytics to gain a competitive advantage for the future. Revealing that community colleges pretend to be more data driven than they actually are, Stout challenges leadership teams to set clear goals, define what success looks like, and ask the right questions to get there. By adopting new tools, abandoning legacy systems and relationships, and boldly adopting open source solutions, colleges can turn large quantities of data into business intelligence that drives transformation.

Previously Published Books in *The Futures Series on Community Colleges*

Minding the Dream: The Process and Practice of the American Community College, Second Edition, by Gail O. Mellow and Cynthia M. Heelan

First in the World: Community Colleges and America's Future, by J. Noah Brown

Community College Student Success: From Boardrooms to Classrooms, by Banessa Smith Morest

Re-visioning Community Colleges, by Debbie Sydow and Richard Alfred

Community Colleges on the Horizon: Challenge, Choice, or Abundance, by Richard Alfred, Christopher Shults, Ozan Jaquette, and Shelley Strickland

Unrelenting Change, Innovation, and Risk

Forging the Next Generation of Community Colleges

Daniel J. Phelan

ROWMAN & LITTLEFIELD
Lanham • Boulder • New York • London

Published by Rowman & Littlefield
A wholly owned subsidiary of The Rowman & Littlefield Publishing Group, Inc.
4501 Forbes Boulevard, Suite 200, Lanham, Maryland 20706
www.rowman.com

Unit A, Whitacre Mews, 26-34 Stannary Street, London SE11 4AB

Copyright © 2016 by Daniel J. Phelan

British Library Cataloguing in Publication Information Available

Library of Congress Cataloging-in-Publication Data Is Available

ISBN 978-1-4758-1263-3 (cloth : alk. paper)
ISBN 978-1-4758-2061-4 (pbk : alk. paper)
ISBN 978-1-4758-1264-0 (electronic)

∞ ™ The paper used in this publication meets the minimum requirements of American National Standard for Information Sciences Permanence of Paper for Printed Library Materials, ANSI/NISO Z39.48-1992.

Printed in the United States of America

Contents

List of Figures

Abbreviations and Sailing Terminology

ABBREVIATIONS

AACC	American Association of Community Colleges
ACC	Austin Community College
ACCT	Association of Community College Trustees
ACE	American Council on Education
AQIP	Academic Quality Improvement Project
ATD	Achieving the Dream
CAO	Chief Administrative Officer
CBE	Competency-Based Education
CCSSE	Community College Survey of Student Engagement
CEO	Chief Executive Officer
CFO	Chief Financial Officer
CMS	Course Management System
CQI	Continuous Quality Improvement
CQIN	Continuous Quality Improvement Network
DLEG	Department of Labor and Economic Growth
EBC	Externally-Based Change
EIC	Externally-Initiated Change
ERP	Enterprise Resource Planning
FRIES	Focus, Research, Implement, Evaluate, and Synthesize
GFA	Global Freshman Academy
GRCC	Grand Rapids Community College
HEA	Higher Education Act
HERDI	Higher Education Research and Development Institute

IBB	Interest-Based Bargaining
IBC	Internally-Based Change
IHE	Institutions of Higher Education
IIC	Internally-Initiated Change
IPEDS	Integrated Postsecondary Education Data System
IPO	Initial Public Offering
KPI	Key Performance Indicator
LMC	Lake Michigan College
MCCA	Michigan Community College Association
MOOC	Massive Open Online Course
MVIS	Minimum Variable Innovation System
NCHMS	National Center for Higher Education Management System
NECSS	Northwest Educational Council for Student Success
NEO	New Employee On-boarder
NILIE	National Initiative for Leadership and Institutional Effectiveness
OCS	Organizational Climate Survey
OER	Open Educational Resources
PACE	Personal Assessment of the College Environment
PASI	Presidents Academy Summer Institute
PDCA	Plan-Do-Check-Act
PSO	Public Service Organization
QEP	Quality Enhancement Plan
RFP	Request for Proposal
SAIL	Strategy Archtype for Innovation and Leading
SACS	Southern Association of Colleges and Schools
SNHU	Southern New Hampshire University
SPC	Strategic Planning Council
STEM	Science, Technology, Engineering, and Math
SWOT	Strengths, Weaknesses, Opportunities, and Threats
TA	Teaching Assistant

TCC	Tidewater Community College
TCS^2	Total Commitment to Student Success
VCCS	Virgina Community College System
USDOE	United States Department of Education
UW	University of Wisconsin
VUCA	Volatility, Uncertainty, Complexity, and Ambiguity
VOIP	Voice over Internet Protocol
WCC	Waubonese Community College
WGU	Western Governors University

SAILING TERMINOLOGY

Batten	An elongated strip of material within the sail designed to support it
Boom	A large spar that runs along the bottom of the sail used for sail control
Bow	The forward part of the hull of the sailboat
Headsail	A sail set forward of the leading mast
Jib	A triangular sail that sits forward of the mainsail
Jibe	A turn wherein the stern of the boat passes through the eye of the wind
Lines	Also called rope, sheets, and halyards depending upon specific use
Mainsail	A large sail located behind the main mast of the boat
Mast	A tall, vertical spar designed to carry one or more sails aloft
Nautical Chart	A representation of shoreline and seafloor, and aids to navigation
Plot	The notation of points or lines on a nautical chart
Rudder	A vertical plate located at the stern of the boat and used for steering
Solution	A calculation of projected course and distance to a new point
Spinnaker	A lightweight sail used for lighter wind conditions and sailing courses
Stern	The very back of the sailboat

Swell	The relative height of waves about the surrounding sea level
Tack	A bow turn that changes the wind from one side of the boat to the other

Foreword

One of the great innovations in American history is the creation of community colleges. For more than a century, our country has benefited from the impact of two-year institutions of higher education. Community colleges deliver educational opportunity to almost half of American undergraduates and more than half of the nation's first-generation college students. They serve as transfer institutions for students matriculating to universities, provide students training and skills leading to jobs and careers that meet business and industry needs, strengthen the middle class, and support a highly diverse student body with equally diverse needs and expectations.

In spite of being ensconced in many traditions of higher education, community colleges are often characterized as innovative, comprehensive, flexible, accessible, and affordable. While author Daniel J. Phelan recognizes the critical role that community colleges have played in our country's advancement, he urges readers to move beyond the successes of the past and recognize that today's community colleges are grappling with a confluence of dynamics that are potentially placing community colleges at the edge of a precipice. Because increased demands for accountability, learning outcomes, transparency, innovation, and competition are accompanied by decreasing levels of federal, state, and local funding support, community colleges are in the midst of tremendous change that requires a commensurate response. In other words, what has made community colleges successful in the past will not make community colleges successful in the future.

As the president and CEO of the League for Innovation in the Community College, I have the privilege of working for an organization—as the name implies—that focuses on identifying, incubating, and disseminating innovative and transformational community college practices, programs, and models, while conducting change and trends research. In the most recent League for Innovation Trends Report (2015), community college presidents, chancellors, and CEOs who were surveyed cited systemic change, risk taking, innovation, and institutional culture as critical areas for deeper understanding and response. In his book, seasoned president Dan Phelan delivers an engaging firsthand perspective on the issues, challenges, and opportunities that community college leaders cited as mission critical from the Trends Report.

In the following chapters, which outline how unrelenting change affects community colleges, Phelan provides insights and guidance for navigating the changing dynamics that influence organizational culture, innovation, and transformational change. Moreover, Phelan charts a series of bold course corrections calling for community college leaders to rethink how innovation and risk influence their work, their institutions, and, ultimately, the students and communities they serve. Specifically, Phelan examines and describes multiple definitions of innovation, including disruptive innovation, and explores the dimensions and interplay of risk, change, and innovation.

A critical issue of unrelenting change that coincides with the critical issues addressed in Phelan's book is the dramatic leadership turnover that community colleges are experiencing and will continue to experience over the next decade. At all institutional levels, these leadership transitions have significant implications for preparing the next generation of community colleges and community college leaders. The new generation will experience a very different set of ecosystems that strongly influence the direction of community colleges. For example, community colleges have ascended into the national spotlight, gleaning notoriety, respect, and support from the federal government, the U.S. Department of Education, and leading foundations—the Bill and Melinda Gates Foundation, the Lumina Foundation, and the Walmart Foundation, just to name a few. As a result, in recent years community colleges have enjoyed unprecedented recognition and support. This newfound recognition and respect are accompanied, however, by higher levels of expectations and accountability that bring to bear greater leadership and cultural pressures, including demands for higher student completion rates, greater transparency, and continued affordability, all in the midst of decreasing federal and state allocations.

For community college leaders—presidents, faculty, vice presidents, deans, student services administrators, and support staff—resting on past laurels is not an option. By delving deep into logic models, concept models for institutional change, specific institutional examples, in-depth analysis of cultural change and leadership attributes, and practical recommendations for change initiation and change management, Phelan provides practical insights and usable models that will serve as valuable resources for community college leaders traversing the ever-changing waters of higher education in early twenty-first-century America.

—Gerardo E. de los Santos, President and CEO, League for Innovation in
the Community College

Preface

"Mindless habitual behavior is the enemy of innovation."
—Rosabeth Moss Kanter

Our nation's community colleges, now 115 years of age, are perfectly and uniquely designed to produce the outcomes our students and our community experience today. Our noble mission is insufficient to surmount the rising dissatisfaction with our performance, as expressed by our various publics and constituents.

Their change mandate is now commonplace and direct: Provide increasing levels of support for increasing numbers of students, of increasing diversity, at higher levels of quality and success, all at a reduced cost; failure to do so will result in decreasing support. The public's required transparency to observe innovation and productivity, as well as the accountability for the dollars expended, are conveyed through legislation, performance-based state support, denied local tax support, student and employer dissatisfaction, and student migration to other providers of higher education. Community colleges do not enjoy the luxury of ignoring this directive.

Barriers that preclude our response—some of our own making, real or perceived—are unacceptable in our technology-driven, on-demand, uberized, participant-centric, shared economy. Unless we embrace this new environment, we will undoubtedly become less and less relevant to more and more people who will have their educational and training needs met elsewhere.

To redesign our community colleges to compete in this changed reality will require an "all-in" approach from all corners of the organization, as the magnitude of the work needed to be achieved cannot be left to presidents and boards of trustees. Such work must first include the organizational and cultural readiness for change, as well as establish a process model for innovation, its implementation, success, and reliability.

To that end, I've designed this book to assist community college boards of trustees, presidents, senior administrators, department chairs, and faculty leaders with transformational change by clarifying what innovation is and is not; how it is different from the media and promotional literature's portrayal, misuse, and devaluation of its meaning; its multiple effects upon organizational culture; and how to deploy change and innovation practices successfully in your organization. Change affecting community colleges is fueled by a tiring multitude of unrelenting forces, including the following:

- declining resources
- institutional life cycle
- competing organizational and community values
- changing regional demographics
- economic conditions
- private, for-profit expansion
- reduced federal, state, and local support
- expanding transparency requirements
- value-proposition justification
- expanding worker training and retraining needs
- growing community expectations
- student self-advocacy
- taxpayer fatigue
- productivity-based funding systems
- rising incivility
- competition
- international opportunities and threats
- ephemeral trust
- shorter technology cycle-times
- an outmoded business model
- recognition that community colleges no longer have the ability to be all things to all people

These, and other conditions like them, have brought to the forefront a clarion decree that community college leaders cannot ignore. The nature of leadership; organizational design; decision-making architecture; board functionality; and operational systems, processes, and protocols that brought community colleges through their first century of existence are woefully insufficient for the next decade, let alone the next hundred years. Furthermore, the public's tolerance of our gradual accretion of knowledge and creation of responsive innovative practices is waning rapidly. Community colleges are at risk.

This book is structured to guide you, the reader, through a logical, provocative, and workable approach to understanding, navigating, and implementing change at your community college. Chapter 1 presents a discussion of change, innovation, and risk/reward relationships. In addition, it introduces key change and innovation terminology used throughout this text by incorporating logic models and a few institutional examples. The section concludes with a discussion of change avoidance issues, a few interesting and promising practices, as well as a review of the work of the American Association of Community Colleges' 21st-Century Commission.

Chapter 2 reviews key theories and research regarding change and innovation, particularly Clayton Christensen's sustaining and disruptive innovation. Additionally, the chapter explores contemporary issues and opportunities related to innovation for community colleges, particularly with regard to their status as paradoxical organizations with competing goals. The chapter further advocates that community colleges should be intentional in pushing beyond traditional decision-making and planning structures to embrace innovation through aggressive environmental scanning, research, and development.

Chapter 3 introduces a concept model for institutional change—the Strategy Archetype for Implementation and Learning (SAIL). The SAIL model illustrates practices essential for the introduction and advancement of change and innovation. The chapter also includes an evidence-based approach to understanding the attributes of leaders and organizations that have successfully pursued innovation. Tools that can be used to determine if a college is ready to pursue innovation based upon its opportunity or threat assessment are presented, as well as strategies for improving the likelihood of success when a decision to innovate has been made.

Chapter 4 focuses upon cultural considerations, which all leaders must take into account when contemplating direction-setting change strategies. Examples are presented wherein institutional culture and subcultures were either ignored or discounted, often resulting in innovation failure. The chapter further explores 1) the dynamics of socialization as a learning and adjustment process within institutions; 2) the value of regular cultural audits for assessing, understanding, and monitoring organizational culture; 3) the implications of competing values within the organization; and 4) the specific ways in which community college leaders can strengthen a culture of openness to change, experimentation, and innovation.

In chapter 5, strategies for preparing a college to advance toward innovation are discussed. Specific institutional examples are offered, including Valencia College in Florida and Rio Salado College in Arizona, which are both known for their prowess in organizational achievement and advancement. This chapter not only describes various organizational models and planning components for innovation, but also reviews the use of data and full disclosure for evaluating the upside and downside of innovation. The chapter also addresses the utility of cost/benefit and risk/rewards analyses, and development of a clear exit strategy should intended goals no longer be achievable.

Chapter 6 examines community colleges that seem not only to survive, but actually to thrive in an environment of continuous change, and to anticipate its arrival. This chapter also provides the reader with an indepth analysis of the leadership attributes necessary for successful innovation. The chapter discussion concludes with a review of best practice implications and provides practical recommendations for campus leaders on change initiation and management.

The concluding afterword, entitled "Forward, Ever Forward," considers the practical realities of change and innovation. It summarizes key messages and describes how leaders can assess existing conditions, chart a new course of action, and sustain buy-in from others in order to achieve success in the long term.

MY APPROACH

Beyond the chapters summarized previously, this book also describes a professional journey that I have undertaken to advance change and innovation in community colleges, a movement to which I have dedicated my career. My personal views and experiences are amplified through research, observations of the practical experiences of my community college colleagues, and visits to hundreds of community colleges across the country over the past thirty-five years.

I have chosen to write this book because, in my view, we have lost our way in terms of bringing our best selves to the work of leading innovation and change in community colleges. I believe that we need to restore the inquisitiveness and pioneering spirit that once defined us.

We need to stop playing it safe and, rather, choose to embrace the discomfort brought on by what is happening and what is yet to come. We must get off the ropes, get on the offense, and do what we know we need to do in the service of others.

In many cases, we should be breaking current models in favor of worthwhile, possibly risky opportunities, refusing to be content with modest gains in student success. Mine is a call to action to be more than we are—to honor the sacrifice and pledge of our progenitors.

I was also prompted to write this book as a supplement to the literature about change and innovation, and to do so from an angle not previously examined. I seek to put the tools of the change process into the hands of practitioners, believing that all of us as community college leaders can do this essential work.

Many of the books I read about change in higher education, though very interesting, are theoretical or needlessly complex in approach. As a college president, I consider these theories a great guide to our understanding. However, the realities of having "boots on the ground" in moments of change and innovation are often different than corresponding operational hypotheses and theoretical constructs. I therefore aim to provide community college leaders with a book that is candid, thought-provoking, informed by practice, but most importantly, that provides replicable tools.

Finally, throughout the book, I continue to use my experience with sailing as a metaphor for components of change and innovation because I find such a strong correlation between the two, and, frankly, it's fun for me to think about sailing as I write this book during a particularly cold Michigan winter.

There are skills and characteristics vital for success as a sailor that align with those of any community college leader intent on having a meaningful and lasting impact. The increasing mandate for change in our industry mirrors a growing storm upon the seas. Grappling with it, respecting it, coping with it, learning from it, and working within its many dimensions are the works of all good captains.

It is my hope that, upon reading this book, institutional leaders will not only better understand our changing community college environment, but also be better able to read approaching and changing conditions, anticipate them, make full use of them, and dare to innovate their way through them. I hope you enjoy the voyage.

Acknowledgments

I offer my sincere thanks to co-editors Drs. Richard Alfred and Debbie Sydow, for their kind invitation to write this book. I am especially thankful for their counsel, guidance, and coaching along the way. Their expert editing on the manuscript made this work even better. I am indebted to them both.

Thanks are also due to my oldest daughter Katie, who amid her other work and life demands, while living in Ireland, took the time to extensively edit this work. I am grateful for her considerable writing and editorial talent. Perhaps the luck of the Irish will go forward with all who read it!

I thank the good ship and crew of Jackson College, particularly the Board of Trustees for their tutelage, guidance, and support of this president, their willingness to risk, and their desire for an innovative community college dedicated to student success. I offer thanks also to the college's Leadership Council with whom I have the distinct pleasure of working each day, as well as the rest of the administration, faculty, and staff that make Jackson College a special place. Thanks also to Dotty Karkheck for her help with graphics for the book.

Extraordinary thanks belong to my wife, Adriana, my sailing companion through many ports. We continue to learn and adapt together to the changing winds and tides. I thank her for her help, support, encouragement, as well as for her ideas and suggestions in our many discussions about this book. I greatly appreciate her edits of the manuscript and technical support of many early drafts. Eu te amo!

I thank also my father- and mother-in-law, Rodolfo and Vania Rasche, who sail with us regularly. I also appreciate our occasional crew as well, daughters Katie, Michelle, Maggie, and Isabella, as I am blessed by their support, encouragement, and acceptance of the time I committed to this book. I am specifically gratful to Katie, who spent many hours helping to edit and refine this book. And especially, I thank my parents, Pat and Janet Phelan, who raised my three younger sisters and me in the Tall Grass Prairie Region of Iowa. We learned of adaptability, flexibility, creativity, problem solving, discipline, ingenuity, and innovation from them, our first teachers.

Note: All revenue that I receive from the sale of this book will be used to provide for student need-based scholarships at Jackson College.

Daniel J. Phelan

ONE

Of Innovation and Possibility

"Learning and innovation go hand in hand. The arrogance of success is to think that what you did yesterday will be sufficient for tomorrow."
—William Pollard

My wife, Adriana, and I love to sail, so much so that throughout the winter months, and well into the early springtime, we talk about sailing, we read about sailing, and we dream about sailing. And when the warmer temperatures return to lower Lake Michigan, we splash the sailboat, select a destination, plot a course solution, and off we go.

Sailing is not only enjoyable and relaxing, it also accords us the excitement of voyaging to some new port and the thrill of finding new realms. But despite the personal renewal and joy we take from it, sailing is first and foremost about achieving a specific objective while addressing a constantly changing set of conditions.

In more ways than you might initially imagine, captaining a sailboat is analogous to serving as a leader of a community college, a company, non-profit, or just about any organization for that matter. The captain is in command of a vessel designed and built for a specific purpose, and ideally brings a vision, a plan, provisions, personal resolve, data, comparative intelligence, a capable crew, training, technology, and the ability to adapt to changing environmental conditions.

Optimally, all of these considerations are brought to bear in advancing the boat toward a particular destination or goal. However, as with any type of leadership, sometimes your plans and related effort don't work out as you had intended; in fact, sometimes they end badly. Perhaps it's an unanticipated development or threat, or perhaps initial planning wasn't as extensive as it might have been.

As though a portend to this reality, I recall an "old salty" telling me some years ago that sailing only looks easy, elegant, and efficient, but in

1

truth, it is a risky proposition of transportation at best. The boat is off course nearly all the time due to a wide variety of uncontrollable and fluctuating factors that impact the good ship and crew, and which constantly require corrective actions. In sailing, multiple irrepressible forces abound. Sound familiar?

As in sailing, change is a constant and, for the most part, an uncontrollable part of an organization's life cycle—and of the human condition in general. Every organization and every individual experiences change, though we may try to struggle against it, or attempt to avoid it—particularly the stresses, anxieties, and tensions that often accompany the change process.

I routinely find that most of us overestimate our ability to affect, control, or circumvent change, or even to change successfully. On some personal level, we may believe that we can and will change, and we may carry that belief with us to our organizations. We may initiate some change in the lives of our organizations, but quite often, organizational inertia, lack of personal commitment, competing priorities or value systems, or insufficient levels of energy required to maintain the new direction prove too difficult to overcome.

Consequently, we *choose* to slide back into old, comfortable ways. As leaders, simply commanding employees to carry out a particular change effort does not necessarily mean that they will follow through, complete, and sustain the effort.

Those who seek to implement change, at whatever organizational level, will "inevitably meet some resistance, even from those who verbally and logically support the change. Change often requires people to step out of their comfort zones, and this may cause certain individuals or groups to resist in order to prevent change from moving forward. When things get difficult, people often go back to things that worked in the past."[1] However, simply conceding this reality and adopting a "that's just the way it is" attitude is insufficient for the future, if an organization is going to be successful.

Whereas changing, for either personal or organizational reasons, used to be an inconsistent undertaking, fraught with fear and abiding disruption, it is now considered a necessary, tactical, and strategic necessity for personal growth, as well as for organizational competitiveness and advancement.

Today, "stability is interpreted more often as stagnation than steadiness, and organizations that are not in the business of change and transition are generally viewed as recalcitrant. The frightening uncertainty that traditionally accompanied major organizational change has been superseded by the frightening uncertainty now associated with staying the same."[2] The status quo cannot be the goal if organizations are not only going to survive, but thrive.

Change comes from a variety of places—not always of our making, not always according to our rules, not always structured around our preferred framework, nor in our ideal time frame. The bottom line to this discussion is that none of us can control very much. Despite our best laid plans, pro-forma budgets, long-term forecasting, theories and predictions, and expectations, there are far too many variables (e.g., people, behaviors, organizational cultures and subcultures, economics, organizational life spans, climate, laws, competition, disease, wars, politics) involved in change to accurately predict outcomes and channel the effects of change to personal or organizational advantage.

Colleges and universities have not staked out a prophetic high ground from which to negate change or tailor the effects of change, or even to prepare for it. Still, leaders and institutions continue to strain to get ahead of the change curve, to leverage it, to do more and better.

This belief-in-action can result in a dizzying pace of intentionally induced changes, in part to succeed, but also to anticipate and adapt to a continuously changing environment. To be sure, intentional change has its upside and downside, but it is altogether necessary if institutions are to remain innovative and competitive over the long term. The implications for leaders are clear: To advance their organizations, they must understand change, appreciate its potential, and most importantly, learn to work within its varied dimensions and constructs.

THE LEXICON OF CHANGE

Before proceeding further, let us clarify terminology used throughout this book. First, for my overarching definition of change, I borrow from University of Michigan's Ross School of Business Clinical Professor of Management and Organization Jeff DeGraff, and the Managing Partner for LIFT Consulting Shawn E. Quinn, in their book *Leading Innovation: How to Jump Start Your Organization's Growth Engine*. The authors suggest that change is an "altered state of an individual or organization produced by both purposeful and unintentional transformational forces."[3] Said another way, change is the process of becoming different, or a different state of being from that which existed prior to the effects of various forces.

To further elucidate the discussion about change, I incorporate the use of a graphical representation (as shown in figure 1.1) developed from a thirty-five-year career in higher education. More specifically, I have experienced change in two broad dimensions: externally-initiated change (EIC) and internally-initiated change (IIC).

EICs are those aspects of life and work that come at us and that are unintentional on our part, sometimes undesirable, and over which we have no control. For example, consider a stock market drop of four hundred points that affects the college's investments, a cancer diagnosis, or the federal government's discontinuation of year-round Pell funding for students. As another practical, yet unprecedented example, consider that in the early months of 2015, Arizona's two largest community colleges, Maricopa and Pima Community College districts, were denied all state financial support due to a political budget deal between the state's governor and legislative leaders.[4]

In the two examples, you may challenge my assertion about lack of control by suggesting that a person can influence legislation through lobbying, and you would be correct. However, ultimately, a lobbyist is not the final decision-maker regarding the legislation. Someone else, or some group, is in control of the final outcome.

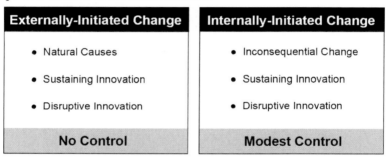

Figure 1.1.   Dimensions of Change and Innovation

Examining the model further, you will note that within the EIC category, three types of change classifications commonly occur: natural causes, "incremental" or sustaining innovation, and disruptive innovation. *Natural causes* of change represent actions that result from events outside of human control, or "acts of God," such as Hurricane Katrina which passed southeast of New Orleans in 2005 and devastated a number of Louisiana community colleges. Other examples might include a campus building fire, a breakout of influenza in student housing, or a gas line break prompting the evacuation of a classroom building.

The remaining EIC classifications are borrowed from Clayton Christensen, the Harvard University professor and author who coined them. *Incremental or sustaining innovation,* hereinafter *sustaining innovation,* is characterized by minor required improvements upon existing operational processes, services, or products.

Though modest in nature, such improvements have the potential to interrupt current modes of practice. While these enhancements provide clear evidence of change, they yield little in the way of significant operational or market gain.[5] Consider, for example, the federal mandate to change the definitions and types of data collected for the Integrated Post-secondary Education Data System (IPEDS). The new definitions and data classifications may more accurately describe the types of students a college serves, but they will not impact the way students are served, the way resources are deployed, or improve the likelihood of student success.

On the other hand, the final EIC classification, *disruptive innovation*, involves change of the highest order of magnitude. It is defined by a radical departure from the methods and structures that are used to conduct business currently and has the potential for revolutionizing organizational success.

These innovations typically begin outside of the industry mainstream, typically involve new actors, and are often inadequate initially, even considered inferior or awkward, compared to the current market methodologies. However, the market is willing to contend with these challenges in favor of the new benefits that accrue to the new product or service—it is viewed as an acceptable tradeoff.[6]

Consider, for example, the introduction of personal digital technology such as the Apple iPad, Microsoft Surface, or large-screen cell phones, sometimes referred to as "phablets." These technologies originated outside the industry of higher education, yet have the potential to provide portable worldwide access to open educational resources (OERs) and instructional materials, and could eventually eliminate the need for textbooks—an occurrence that will lower educational costs and introduce new markets.

I further propose that internally-initiated change (IIC), in contrast to externally-initiated change (EIC), is characterized by direct and intentional action within the organization. It occurs when something is done to alter a process, service, or outcome. Within this category, there are three classifications of change, two of which share name and general character with their counterparts in EIC: inconsequential change, sustaining innovation, and disruptive innovation.

I refer to *Inconsequential Change* as those actions within institutions that are not innovative nor particularly creative; they are simply different states of being. Examples include the relocation of staff and faculty offices to accommodate building renovations, the purchase of electric cars for the college motor pool to replace traditional combustible engine vehicles, or the installation of a new campus-wide telephone system using Voice over Internet Protocol (VoIP). Each of these examples is a change that does not impact the mission and core values of the organization.

The remaining two IIC innovation classifications, *sustaining innovation* and *disruptive innovation*, differ from the EIC categories only in that they are intentionally derived from, and occur internally within, the organization.

As these categories and classifications of change suggest, a key strategy for organizational competitiveness, as well as anticipating and responding to change, is innovation.

Innovation, as defined by DeGraff and Quinn, is the "intentional development of products, services, processes, or expressions, such as design and fashion, which results from organizational and individual creativity, as well as intentional and unintentional discovery."[7] As a slight adjustment to this definition, I argue, based upon personal experience, and as noted previously, that innovation can be either internally or externally initiated.

In any case, leaders can sit back, let change happen and react to its effects, or they can be proactive about it. Passivity may be safe and prudent—a seemingly sound strategy when weighed against spending scarce resources on change that is uncertain or unproven. But leaders must actively choose to pursue innovation if they wish to have any role in shaping the institution's destiny, instead of leaving it to outside forces. This choice requires thoughtful and intentional action.

COMMUNITY COLLEGES AND INNOVATION

From the point of their creation, the junior college and, later, the "community college," served as the point of entry for the masses to pursue postsecondary education. They provided an opportunity to obtain a credential of market value that could stand on its own, or be leveraged toward a baccalaureate degree.

Community colleges were themselves a bona fide disruptive innovation on the higher education landscape. They stepped into a void, a learner market not addressed by educational entities of the day. Community colleges have always been bastions of creativity, innovation, market adaptation, risk taking, and resourcefulness in a change-averse industry.[8] Still, their early development was not assured, nor was it realized without trial.

The potential of community colleges was embedded in what traditional institutions of higher learning *would not* do, as well as what a new breed of institutions *would* do. Community colleges quickly developed a reputation for anticipating and responding to the changing needs of those for whom they were established to serve.

Their original three-pronged mission of transfer education, career education, and community service positioned them to innovate in program and service delivery unencumbered by the organizational and cultural structures of their competitors. Their mission, vision, and values spurred both incremental and disruptive innovation in response to local, regional, state, and national needs by, for example, educating returning war veterans, introducing new technologies, and promoting regional economic development.

During the first decades of their development, community colleges broke the rules of the game. They stood apart because of their irreverence toward the way things had always been done before, choosing instead to

commit to service, and to provide access to higher education for everyone.

Despite this incredible innovative beginning, it seems that the community college's capacity for creative and entrepreneurial zeal has diminished as thought and action have become more closely aligned with traditional, mainstream higher education. Indeed, community colleges are not
breaking the rules as they once did. Instead, the latest innovations in
higher education come from public and private universities.

Consider, for example, the creation of massive open online courses
(MOOCs), competency-based education (CBE) credentialing, and subscription enrollment modeling—each one led by universities. Community college leaders are playing it safe, and our ability to aggressively
pursue goals, address the changing environment, and innovate has
waned. This is of deep concern, and it suggests a possible shift along the
organizational life cycle of the industry.

Without question, community colleges today are faced with intensifying expectations set against stationary or declining financial resources
with which to accomplish all that is being asked of them—the same is
true of higher education generally. For many institutional leaders, the
thought of being innovative while concurrently limited by financial constraints is a journey too far.

Relative to organizational life cycle, University of Michigan Ross Business School Professor Kim Cameron notes, "As a result of their concern
with fiscal problems, many institutions of higher education have developed characteristics and have pursued strategies that seem to be resilien-
cy-inhibiting rather than resiliency-enhancing. That is, they have operated in ways during times of prosperity and abundance that have made it
difficult to respond effectively to conditions resulting from a changing
environment."[9]

This stagnancy may, in part, explain the rising public clamor regarding low rates of student success, rising costs, and marginal outcomes.
Global and national competitive forces, when combined with evolving
consumer needs and demands, require disruptive approaches to positioning the community college as a distinguished provider of high-quality continuous education. We must therefore return to the innovative,
aggressive, forward-thinking strategies of our community college progenitors. Unfortunately, the timing for this to happen could not be worse.
An accelerating pace of change in market demand and rising consumer
expectations are now juxtaposed to a diminished aspiration for change
and innovation.

The ability and wherewithal to innovate is an essential skill for community college leaders, and it must be deeply rooted and cultivated in an
institution's planning processes and ethos. That said, "the hierarchical
structures and organizational processes we have used for decades to run
and improve our enterprises are no longer up to the task of winning in

this faster-moving world. In fact, they can actually thwart attempts to compete in a marketplace where discontinuities are more frequent and innovators must always be ready to face new problems . . . any [organization] that isn't rethinking its direction every few years—as well as constantly adjusting to change contexts—and then quickly making significant operation changes is putting itself at risk."[10]

Thus, community colleges must establish new organizational structures and processes that enable them to anticipate, leverage, and pursue new and emerging opportunities. In turn, leaders must fully understand the nature of change and its implications for individuals and the organization, as well as its effects upon the culture of the institution. Additionally, leaders must remain hypervigilant of industry threats and the changing landscape of higher education, as well as work aggressively to acquire and develop talent that can welcome and drive change.

While leaders may choose to develop new structures, protocols, rubrics and leadership skills for advancing change in the organization, it is important to remember that leaders must also hone their skills in situational assessment, adaptability, and discipline to cope with unforeseen challenges. Like the sailor, keep an eye toward the horizon, and once the winds of change hit, you must be ever ready to embrace the opportunity or threat and make the best possible speed to the new destination, ever mindful of associated risk.

In grappling with change, I have found it helpful to perceive it along a continuum upon which risk and reward are correlated (as shown in figure 1.2). At one end is incremental or sustaining change, which accrues limited benefits to the organization and is marked by limited risk, modest distraction, and an easy pathway to acceptance. At the opposite end of the spectrum is the potential for substantial performance gain through disruptive innovation. Change of this type is palpable and significant in the life of the organization and its personnel. It is marked by new systems, new products, fresh strategies and practices, and new market potential.

To extend the sailing metaphor further, this level of innovation is analogous to the addition of an asymmetrical spinnaker (a very large, light, colorful sail, sometimes called a "kite," that balloons out in front of the sailboat) in addition to the two traditional sails (the mainsail and headsail/jib). The spinnaker has the potential to capitalize upon lighter winds and wind angles, thereby allowing the sailboat to operate in a greater number of varying wind conditions. Its use requires additional lines for handling, a new level of understanding of performance characteristics, deployment and recovery methods, as well as an overarching knowledge of safety and maintenance.

Unless the crew is given an opportunity to provide input into the decision to acquire such a sail, as well as participate in training on the use of a spinnaker and its installation, there is a higher likelihood of resis-

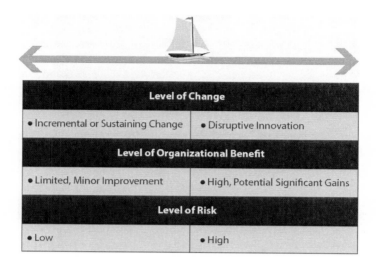

Figure 1.2.   Change Continuum

tance to being drawn out of their comfort zone, to say nothing of the potential for personal injury.

As DeGraff and Quinn put it, "the more significant the transformation, the more likely there will be greater resistance from key stakeholders. This means that maintaining a positive relationship with the initiative's sponsor and allowing enough time to develop buy-in from other key stakeholders is of paramount importance."[11] Inaction or inattention to any of these challenges and associated risks can result in suboptimal outcomes, and a conclusion that the pursuit of innovation is a bad idea and a waste of time and resources.

CHANGE AND RISK

Change happens through leaders, in concert with the governing board and the core leadership team, who in turn work through others to pivot the institution. Insofar as top leaders cannot work apart from the institutional transformation process, they must engage in critical self-evaluation to determine whether or not they have the interest, courage, and skills necessary to lead change.

Second, and just as importantly, leaders must discern whether their staff have the appetite and capacity for disruption, and whether they can move beyond existing practices, policies, culture, and the "the way we've always done it" mentality. Richard Alfred, Christopher Shults, Ozan Jaquette, and Shelley Strickland note that "often what prevents institutions from achieving their full potential is not competencies or resources, but missed opportunity. Leaders look at the future through the lens of the present and, in so doing, undercut their institutions' capability for growth and change. A sense of possibility is as important as a sense of foreboding in inducing a college to change." [12]

Avoidance of change carries its own set of risks, which shape institutional destiny through default—it's what a college doesn't do that defines what it will become. All organizations have personnel who are living in the "avoidance space." They have been lulled into believing that things are fine as they are, that there is no reason or urgency to change how things are done.

Even more concerning is the perceived operational imperative "that is not merely 'if it ain't broke, don't fix it' but rather 'even if it is broke, it's better than what a fix might bring'—the constraint you know is better than the opportunity you do not know. As a consequence, some campus leaders prefer doing nothing as an acceptable alternative to change of any kind. If campus groups can make the campus stick to present circumstances, they thwart change they cannot control. Isolation from external pressures makes this possible by diminishing the sense of urgency about change that those who are better connected may feel." [13]

To combat this isolation, a college can engage employees through numerous communications describing the need for change: newsletters, PowerPoint presentations, graphs, benchmarking data, convocations, invited speakers, and employee meetings. Still, staff all too often remain in disbelief, as the status quo seems safe, functional, and comfortable. Indeed, as validation of this position, employees see that the college is continuing to enroll students, faculty are teaching in their classrooms, bills are being paid, students are graduating, the community is being served, and the doors are still open.

Yet forces inside and outside the higher education industry are demanding a response. In addition to these pressures, consider the concomitant development and introduction of customized learning pathways, the commoditization of higher education, micro-degrees, tuition-zero community colleges, the growth of competency-based education, the unbundling of educational services, social broadcasting, increasing accreditation requirements, and the abundance of free and OERs. These forces provide additional evidence of the primacy of change that cannot be ignored.

An interesting and disruptive initiative with explicit irreverence toward tradition is the Thiel Fellowship, established by Peter Thiel. An entrepreneur, venture capitalist, and co-founder of PayPal, Thiel offers to pay students under the age of twenty *not* to go to college, offering them $100,000 over two years to do something interesting with their lives, such as pursing their own research or starting a business.

This initiative flows from Thiel's publicly stated concerns regarding the questionable value of a college education. He suggests a high likelihood that we will soon face a "higher education bubble" that prompts the demise of our industry as we now know it.[14] Thiel, who has been correct on a number of his prognostications regarding technologies and housing bubbles, may well be right.

As additional proof of his insight and vision, consider that in the four years since the program began, eighty-three participating fellows have incubated new companies that have raised over seventy-two million dollars in investments, and resulted in over twenty-nine million in net revenue.[15] It's advisable then to suspend judgment long enough to at least consider the possibility that he may have found one of many viable disruptions to higher education, rather than dismissing this paradigm-breaking innovation with a belief that Thiel is just an uniformed, undisciplined billionaire.

The consideration of new and innovative ideas, let alone the recognition of a national change mandate for higher education, is often harshly judged because it comes from people outside of our industry and because much of public higher education is in disagreement with it. Often our vision is narrow, and our blind spots become opportunities for others to exploit.

The role of faculty, in particular, as instructional experts may, in fact, further hinder our ability to see new possibilities. Daniel Rowley, Herman Lujan, and Michael Dolence note that "faculty are, by role and ability, experts. Experts do not heed others well. Expertise, a bias for tradition, protection offered by existing process, and insulation from external pressures all engrain themselves in faculty instincts. This condition is reinforced by the basic skepticism that is endemic to deliberation before making a judgement. Instincts buttressed by scholarly methods lead to an inertia that is not easily reversed."[16]

It is improper to suggest that faculty alone are complacent in thought and action, as the challenge is both institutional and industry-wide.

> The current crisis in today's [colleges] is real, and much of it is of the [colleges'] own making. In the spirit of honoring tradition, [colleges] hang on to past practices to the point of imperiling their futures. When reduced budgets force them to cut costs, they trim but rarely make hard tradeoffs . . . paradoxically, they respond to economic downturn by raising prices. From a market competition standpoint, it is slow institutional suicide. It is as if [colleges] do not care about what is going on around them or how they are perceived.[17]

It is fair to state then that if community colleges are to move beyond the status quo either in response to a rapidly changing environment or of a desire to be innovative and competitive, a new paradigm for our industry is needed.

This is not to say that all change is necessarily positive. As institutional leaders, we must be mindful that our efforts toward change and innovation can create unintended consequences. Consider, for example, the enduring challenge that developmental education has created for community college leaders. The majority of incoming community college students possess insufficient skills in at least one core subject area, most often mathematics.

Nationally, it is well known that over 60 percent of new student cohorts are not ready for collegiate-level work.[18] If an incoming student's skill assessment results indicate that he or she requires remediation in math, the likelihood that the student will complete developmental math courses and advance to college-level or "gateway" credit courses is about 30 percent nationally. The statistics are far worse for students who test into remedial education in two or more foundational areas, and more so for students of color or students from a low socioeconomic background. Their likelihood of success is near zero.

Many community colleges have mandated enrollment in developmental courses and programs because we believe that foundational skill-building is the right thing to do, and we have found that students "don't do optional." So we drive them to work on their fundamental skills to improve the likelihood of their success. However, the painful truth is that developmental education is a dead zone for students.

The conversation and rationale around this issue universally include comments such as: 1) Students are not getting the education they should have had in high school; 2) Students are not motivated to succeed; 3) There are not enough resources available to advance a student from testing at third-grade math levels to college-level in a reasonable period of time; 4) Students should have the right to fail; 5) Our data look bad because we have to accept all students, while other colleges and universities do not; 6) The parents are at fault; and 7) This is just the way it is, and there is nothing we can do to change things.

We develop blended courses, introduce supplemental instructors, add tutors, pursue grants, buy more software for self-paced instruction, and purchase diagnostic assessments so students don't need to take the entirety of a developmental sequence. And we keep trying. At some point, as institutional leaders, we need to stop the madness of this present work. The educational casualties are simply too many.

The Virginia Community College System (VCCS) introduced a number of practices that exemplify reimagining the current reality. Leaders at VCCS sought to revamp their developmental education system, beginning with mathematics since it was the largest barrier to success for most students. Rather than employing a universal approach for student placement, the VCCS decided to customize the process by assessing only those areas of math specific to a student's program of study.

Faculty deconstructed the math education components into nine modules for student testing. As Josh Wyner, vice president and executive director of the College Excellence Program at the Aspen Institute, explains, "Only students intending to transfer to a four-year college and major in math and science fields need to be deemed proficient in all nine areas to begin college-level work. Liberal arts majors are only required to demonstrate that they know the first five units, while students entering career and technical programs take assessments in only the basic skills needed for their areas of study."[19]

While there have been promising results, both in terms of the percentage of students not requiring developmental education courses (a 10.5 percent reduction) and students enrolling in college credit mathematics classes (a 12.2 percent increase), the needle of student success has not moved to an optimum level. More work remains.

With President Obama's call for an increase of 50 percent more college graduates by the year 2020, and more states linking student completion rates to state aid support, the likelihood of our helping significantly more students achieve the president's goal seems low. Indeed, the Lumina Foundation reported in 2015 that while there has been some gain associated with increasing postsecondary attainment, the current rate of progress, trending forward, is simply insufficient to achieve its stated goal of 60 percent of Americans in possession of a postsecondary credential by the year 2025.[20]

In 2015 the American Association of Community Colleges projected that collectively, their members will fall just short (i.e., within 10 percent) of reaching their goal to increase student completion rates by 50 percent by 2020.[21] However, this projection assumes that the current velocity and trajectory of completion trends since academic year 2010 will be constant, which seems unlikely given declining national enrollment. Thus, we cannot, and must not, declare victory and forego innovation, as there is much work yet to be done and too many students' lives to positively impact—but how?

THE PROMISE OF THE FUTURE

A small group of higher education organizations is making inroads through innovation. Consider, for example, Southern New Hampshire University (SNHU), a regionally accredited institution that has a crystal clear vision to provide students and employers with a value-added education that builds upon skills students already have, and which is available 24/7 online using a Blackboard learning management platform. Gone is the old academic model.

SNHU does not offer developmental education, semester segmentation, grades, or grade levels. These traditional practices have been replaced by a structure that allows students to advance at their own pace. While they do not earn alphanumeric grades, they do receive a transcript that outlines the particular competencies they possess at the completion of their college journey.

In addition, SNHU has solved the age-old federal financial aid barrier to innovation by working with the U.S. Department of Education to establish a waiver so that SNHU students can receive Pell funding. SNHU has also implemented a top-drawer, individualized customer service strategy and partnered directly with industry to meet specific workforce needs.

As a demonstration of the value SNHU places on continuous quality improvement and their respect for the "voice of the customer," the university regularly asks for student feedback about their experience. One student offered this statement:

> My professors have been timely and extremely knowledgeable, as well as extremely helpful. In my other classroom courses, it was; drive to school, sit in class, listen to lecture with PowerPoint or on chalkboard, drive home (any questions or issues—good luck in scheduling time with the professor or TA, MOST Professors only have limited office hours for student questions or problems), but at SNHU, it was: log in, get comprehensive week course instructions, watch lectures, pause if needed, rewind to review, take notes, do assigned readings and research, review lectures, contact professor for immediate response, post extensive, cited researched discussion posts and replies, write papers and do work, as well as discuss course and questions with other students and professor on discussion boards . . . and repeat the next week. SNHU is NOT easy. It is the most writing and research I have ever done for class work. I would say a great education for the price.[22]

This student's comment perfectly illustrates what an increasing number of community college and university students seek: higher education on their terms, customized to their needs, and at their convenience, not ours. They do not want our traditional fifteen-week semester at days and times that accommodate the schedule of the professor, the institutional master schedule, or the planting and harvesting seasons. They want feedback in a timely fashion, and a lot of it. They want access to information, and they don't understand why colleges cannot give them credit for what they already know. Enter, the opportunity to innovate.

Similar to the visioning and implementation efforts of frame-breaking institutions like SNHU, the American Association of Community Colleges (AACC) embarked on a project in 2011 to map the future of two-year institutions. Following a listening tour across the country, AACC President Walter Bumphus created a blue-ribbon panel, the 21st Century Commission, and charged it with developing a new design for community college education.

The commission was comprised of a Who's Who of community college and university leaders and faculty, numerous community college and higher education association leaders, and business executives. The project was funded by the Kresge Foundation and the Bill and Melinda Gates Foundation.

The commission boldly issued a charge to the field: "If community colleges are to contribute powerfully to meeting the needs of twenty-first century students and the twenty-first century economy, education leaders must reimagine what these institutions are—and are capable of becoming."[23]

As part of the process, opportunities for input were provided at the AACC annual convention, with many other meetings conducted with community college leaders throughout the nation. After more than two years of work by the commission and its various committees, what resulted was a distillation of research, data, narratives, anecdotes, and promising practices, all presented within two documents: *Reclaiming the American Dream—Community Colleges and the Nation's Future,* and *Empowering Community Colleges: To Build the Nation's Future, An Implementation Guide.*

The latter document provides illustrations and tools to help community college leaders with translation and implementation of concepts outlined in the first document, *Reclaiming the American Dream.* The *Empowering* document also presents seven recommendations and attendant strategies, collectively summarized as a call to action designed to "redesign students' educational experiences, reinvent institutional roles, and reset the system to better promote student success."[24]

Ultimately, community colleges across the country, boards, presidents, faculty, and staff were asked to embrace once again that which had defined them for over a hundred years: innovation and dedication to student success.

The implementation guide addresses the need for commitment to sustainable change among practitioners in the field, as well as those interested in being part of the community college movement. Citing implications for presidents and boards of trustees, the report concluded that community colleges must direct their governing boards toward "substantial improvement [that] depends significantly on boards taking seriously their responsibility to create policy conditions necessary to improve student progress and success . . . beginning with hiring CEOs who will lead transformational change and supporting them in doing courageous work."[25] The report implores presidents and chancellors to be "open to new institutional roles and structures, comfortable with data, capable of leading transformational change, and relentlessly focused on equity and student success."[26] Leadership work is at the core of both reports.

Both commission documents are replete with a sense of urgency for change, and they include many examples of how community colleges are adapting. Additionally, and as part of the commission's goal to provide a continuously updated virtual resource for colleges to post and share information, an online AACC 21st-Century Center was created. The website provides recommendations, examples, stories, articles, research, videos, webinars, and opinions about the good work going on at community colleges nationwide. To be sure, the resources and their illustrations of successful institutional practices are a great resource for benchmarking and ideation, and they represent a call to action.

It should be noted, however, from a change process and leadership perspective that it would be irresponsible simply to lift these ideas and bolt them onto institutional operations without due consideration of a specific college's culture, context, risk/reward, and political and financial realities, let alone an institution's willingness to commit to change.

Building an institutional culture of innovation is something beyond mere tweaking of current methods. It requires thoughtful and intentional discussion, strategy, flexibility, preparation, and support with a full measure of patience. Should a college be interested in implementing a practice that is successful at a high-performing institution, it should reach out to that institution and investigate the full magnitude of what worked and did not work, as well as the exemplary college's culture, its challenges, how it overcame obstacles, who was involved, what metrics guided the work, and what success looked like on the ground. Significant organizational change is rarely linear.

Shakespeare's Antonio, in *The Tempest*, notes that the past is prologue for what is to come. The same can be said of community colleges. Like our community college progenitors, I believe that community college leaders, boards, faculty, and staff must recommit themselves to building a change-acclimating culture, aggressively and creatively pursuing solutions through innovation, and delivering personalized instructional pathways and opportunities for students, which lead to success.

Distraction in any of its forms—confusion, conflict, ego, and the like— must be avoided to make room for opportunity. To that end, community colleges will require leaders who are capable of understanding and appreciating the past, while possessing the knowledge, skills, and intuition to navigate the new and often uncharted waters of competition, rapid acceleration of technology, and changing community needs, all while advancing the organization toward new vistas.

Community college leaders must understand the nature of, and be comfortable with, the constantly shifting seas of our industry, with a capacity for understanding whether an idea is a passing fancy or something worthy of careful consideration. To do this, they will need to assess the magnitude and complexity of an opportunity, determine if adoption represents a modest adjustment or a major disruption, evaluate the potential for risk and reward, and properly prepare themselves and their organization for the work that lies ahead.

Leaders will need to "see the whole chessboard" and consider the direct and indirect implications of innovation, as well as the potentially unintended consequences, and arrive at a value-based judgment about whether to pursue the innovation or pass on it. The work will not be easy. There will most assuredly be stiff winds and storms. Colleges, like sailboats, will require a confident, well-trained, steady hand upon the rudder, guiding crew and ship to better shores.

NOTES

1. Jeff DeGraff and Shawn E. Quinn, *Leading Innovation: How to Jump Start Your Organization's Growth Engine* (New York: McGraw-Hill Companies, Inc., 2007), 222.

2. Kim S. Cameron and Robert E. Quinn, *Diagnosing and Changing Organizational Culture, Based on the Competing Values Framework* (San Francisco, CA: Jossey-Bass, 2011), 1.

3. DeGraff and Quinn, *Leading Innovation: How to Jump Start Your Organization's Growth Engine*, 8.

4. Ashley A. Smith, "Zeroed Out in Arizona." *Inside Higher Ed* (March 12, 2015). Accessed on March 16, 2015. https://www.insidehighered.com/news/2015/03/12/arizona-unprecedented-defunding-community-colleges.

5. Clayton M. Christensen, *The Innovator's Dilemma: The Revolutionary National Bestseller That Changed the Way We Do Business.* Rev. and updated ed. (New York: Harper-Business, 2000).

6. Ibid.

7. DeGraff and Quinn, *Leading Innovation: How to Jump Start Your Organization's Growth Engine*, 8.

8. Debbie Sydow and Richard Alfred, *Re-visioning Community Colleges* (Lanham, MD: Rowman & Littlefield Publishers, Inc., 2012).

9. Kim S. Cameron and David A. Whetten, "Models of the Organizational Life Cycle: Applications to Higher Education." *College and University Organization Insights from the Behavioral Sciences.* Bess, James L., Ed. (New York: EXXON Education Foundation, 1984), 33.

10. John P. Kotter, "Accelerate!" *Harvard Business Review* (November 2012), 44–58.

11. DeGraff and Quinn, *Leading Innovation: How to Jump Start Your Organization's Growth Engine*, 68.

12. Richard Alfred, et al., *Community Colleges on the Horizon: Challenge, Choice, or Abundance* (Lanham, MD: Rowman & Littlefield Publishers, Inc., 2009), 5.

13. Daniel James Rowley, Herman D. Lujan, and Michael G. Dolence, *Strategic Change in Colleges and Universities: Planning to Survive and Prosper* (San Francisco, CA: Jossey Bass, Inc., 1997), 77–78.

14. Thiel Fellowship, "About the Fellowship." Accessed October 19, 2014. http://www.thielfellowship.org/.

15. Beth McMurtrie, "The Rich Man's Dropout Club: Whatever Happened to the Teenage Entrepreneurs Whom Peter Thiel Paid to Forgo College?" *The Chronicle of Higher Education.* February 8, 2015. Accessed March 16, 2015. http://chronicle.com/article/The-Rich-Mans-Dropout-Club/151703/#.

16. Rowley, Lujan, and Dolence, *Strategic Change in Colleges and Universities: Planning to Survive and Prosper*, 78.

17. Clayton M. Christensen and Henry J. Eyring, *The Innovative University: Changing the DNA of Higher Education from the Inside Out* (San Francisco: Jossey-Bass, 2011), xxii–xxiii.

18. Thomas Bailey, "Challenge and Opportunity: Rethinking the Role and Function of Developmental Education in Community College." *New Directions for Community Colleges*, 145 (2009), 11–30.

19. Josh S. Wyner, *What Excellent Community Colleges Do: Preparing All Students for Success* (Cambridge, MA: Harvard Education Press, 2014), 50.

20. Lumina Foundation, *A Stronger Nation through Higher Education.* (Indianapolis, IN: Lumina Foundation, 2015), 5.

21. American Association of Community Colleges. "Community College Completion." Accessed April 24, 2015. http://www.aacc.nche.edu/AboutCC/Trends/Documents/completion_nsc_report.pdf.

22. Southern New Hampshire University (SNHU), "Southern New Hampshire University Reviews." Accessed October 19, 2014. http://www.onlinedegreereviews.org/college/southern-new-hampshire-university-reviews/reviews/.

23. American Association of Community Colleges. "Empowering Community Colleges: To Build the Nation's Future, An Implementation Guide. Accessed September 13, 2014. http://www.aacc21stcenturycenter.org/wp-content/uploads/2014/04/EmpoweringCommunityColleges_final.pdf, 3.

24. Ibid.

25. Ibid, 7.

26. Ibid.

TWO

Forms and Dimensions of Change

"He that will not apply new remedies must expect new evils; for time is the greatest innovator."
—Francis Bacon, "Of Innovations," *Essays*, 1815

Change. Disruptive innovation. Transformation. Improvement. Reform. Growth. Enhancement. Restructuring. Development. These words, frequently used interchangeably, suggest a promising future for some. For others, they prompt worry, anxiety, or fear of the loss of all they have known.

It seems natural to want to keep things the way they are because routine is familiar, comfortable, understandable, and safe. Change may be welcome or unwelcome, quick or plodding, helpful or harmful, predictable or unpredictable, orderly or chaotic, modest or life-altering. While there may be many terms associated with change and innovation, caution is advised in the use of these terms, so as to avoid creating havoc in an organization or among employees.

Communication is the principal vehicle by which leaders will educate employees of the need and rationale for impending organizational change. Unfortunately, as Juett Cooper argues, "practitioners and investigators often treat innovation as an all-inclusive term, even though they may be referring to very different events or processes."[1]

Without intentional clarity of language regarding organizational change, leaders may create confusion, at best and at worst, provide fodder for the change resisters who decry the use of euphemisms and consider them subterfuge deployed by administrators to stave off fear and resistance until it is too late. This is one of the chief reasons change is avoided: lack of trust and communication.

The strange truth is that many of us will do just about anything to hang on to what we know, even to our own detriment. Think I'm being dramatic? Consider as an example the statistic that an average of 25 percent of heart attack and stroke victims do not change their health habits, even when doing so would significantly reduce the likelihood of a second episode and extend their lives.[2]

In one study, *The Journal of Clinical Oncology* reported, after studying 9,000 cancer survivors, more than 80 percent chose not to follow the recommendation of consuming five fruits and vegetables per day.[3] These behaviors and related data are enigmatic because they demonstrate that people would rather risk their very lives than accept changes in them.

Change should be, on some level, intuitive. We are born into a foreign world. From childhood we learn to crawl, fall many times, and then walk. We learn to communicate. We advance our independence. We learn new things. We acquire new skills. We get married. We buy the next iPhone and try to figure it out. We take a promotion with more responsibility. We purchase a home. We lose a job. We get a dog. We find a new job. We get a new boss at work. We miss a flight. We grow older.

Indeed, our daily lives are filled with change and significantly influenced by the way we adapt to it. We deal with a lifelong, incessant parade of change, which mostly seems manageable, especially if it comes in measured doses, because we are in control. It's our life and we can make the decisions.

However, in the work environment, people feel more vulnerable because we control variables to a very limited extent, especially if we want to keep our jobs, so reactions to change can more easily descend into frustration. The degree of discomfort and corresponding desire to avoid change intensifies in tandem with feeling undervalued, uninvolved, or uninformed regarding the reasoning for the coming wave of change.

At least one thing about change is universal. The achievement of organizational objectives is dependent upon employees performing their jobs in new ways, to new ends. According to Jeffery Hiatt and Timothy Creasy, "a perfectly designed process that no one follows produces no improvement in performance. A perfectly designed technology that no one uses creates no additional value to the organization. Perfectly defined job roles that are not fulfilled by employees deliver no sustained results. Whether in the workplace, in the community or in government, the bridge between a quality solution and the benefit realization is individuals embracing and adopting the change."[4]

Make no mistake, if change is to occur in our community colleges, it will be through and by personnel. Therefore, "to lead change at an organizational level, you must be able to lead change at an individual level."[5] Undertaking this level of work in our organization is both extensive and complex. Given that the bulk of our community college workplace is comprised of, and our organizational work is conducted by, administration, faculty, and staff, the college's leadership dare not give short shrift to the implications of change as it affects employees.

How employees react to institutional change is dependent upon their relationship with it. When change affects someone else, it is of little concern, yet when change directly affects us, we sound the claxons. Think about it—how many of us have heard about the installation of a new ERP (enterprise resource planning) management software system at the college that seemed like a good idea until it impacted our work personally?

We become bothered by the interruption and the inconvenience, so we complain. Perhaps some of us are so bold as to announce that to spend money on this new technology is frivolous, particularly when money is tight and there is presumably nothing wrong with the current software system, though we might have previously complained about that old system as well.

Not surprisingly, there is a plethora of consultants, speakers, books, websites, and blogs designed to help us manage change in our institutions. In fact, in the course of writing this book, I initiated a Bing search for "managing change at work" that resulted in over 106,000,000 hits, which should indicate something about the nature of change and our need for assistance! But despite countless quick guides to change, YouTube videos about coping with it, and blogs boasting a shortcut to overcome it, the reality is that working with and through change is a multifaceted undertaking.

It's not a checklist, but a process. Done well, a thoughtful and comprehensive change strategy can develop and engage employees, optimize resource utilization, reduce risk, and improve the likelihood of successful outcomes.

Before delving into the realities of change and innovation in community colleges and how best to position our organizations for the future, it is helpful to consider the breadth of the existing research on this topic so as to provide context for the endeavor. Whether the literature hails from higher education, business, or health care, a commonly struck chord is that organizations need to be deliberate and attentive to the process.

CHANGE VERSUS INNOVATION

There are about as many definitions of "change" and "innovation" as there are authors to define them. Quite often, and within the framework of this book, change and innovation are viewed as companion constructs, but in truth they are fundamentally different. Marshal Poole and Andrew Van de Ven describe change as "an empirical observation of difference in form, quality, or state over time in an organizational entity. The entity may be an individual's job, a work group, an organizational strategy, a program, a product, or the overall organization."[6]

Working from a public service organization (PSO) perspective, professors Stephen Osborne and Kerry Brown define change as the "gradual improvement and/or development of the existing services provided by a PSO and/or other organizational context. [Change] represents continuity with the past."[7] And, you will recall, as noted in the introduction, Jeff DeGraff and Shawn Quinn define change as "an altered state of an individual or organization produced by both purposeful and unintentional transformational forces."[8] Taken together, these definitions explain change as the product of the execution of our intentions.

Innovation is something altogether different. Although innovation almost always results in change, not all change is innovative. Osborne and Brown characterize innovation as "the introduction of new elements into a public service—in the form of new knowledge, a new organization, and/or new management or processual skills. It represents discontinuity with the past."[9]

Relatedly, DeGraff and Quinn define innovation as "the intentional development of products, series, processes, or expressions, such as design and fashion, which results from organizational and individual creativity, as well as intentional and unintentional discovery."[10] The League for Innovation in the Community College suggests, based upon its research, that there is no universal definition for innovation. Rather, they offer multiple thoughts, including the idea that "innovation concerns the search for and the discovery, experimentation, development, imitation, and adoption of new products, new processes, and new organizational setups."[11]

To summarize these and other views, consider for the purposes of this book that change, at its most basic level, is an intervention that alters the current state of an organization, culture, product, or service, or virtually anything. Change, by necessity, is the follow-on action to any innovation. Innovation in itself is an inventive, creative, inspired, and intentionally designed process with the specific outcome of organizational and process design improvement, which may contemplate various degrees of organizational and personal disruption. Innovation precedes the change process, as change is the vehicle by which innovation is realized.

Consider the following example as a means to further clarify differences between change and innovation. After reviewing registration data, a community college notices a decline in the number of eighteen- to twenty-four-year-old applicants. A decision is made to target the younger demographic through use of generational messages. The college's marketing department changes its existing message in order to attract younger potential students while maintaining the same traditional media outlets (television, radio, and print media).

Alternatively, the same college could choose to consider broadly the enrollment challenge and expand beyond its traditional promotional strategies. It could, for a start, incorporate multiple social media platforms (e.g., Facebook, Twitter, CafeMom, LinkedIn, Hi5, Livestream, or Instagram) in an effort to attract more youthful students. To achieve this objective, the institution hires a director of social media who concentrates his or her creative work efforts upon current, as well as emerging, social media sites. The director could also develop scalable messages designed for persons who routinely use "phablets" and wearables, and perhaps a new college app as well.

In the first example, the college altered its message. It initiated an action that resulted in a different state. It implemented a change, but it was decidedly noninnovative. In the second example, the college considered new, creative possibilities that involved the addition of social media elements to the college's marketing mix.

The new idea required fresh thinking, invention, and changes in processes, practices, and staffing to realize new outcomes. The ideation was purposeful, creative, and strategic—in a word, innovative. The use of new media, the message design, and the hiring of a director were all changes to institutional practice; they were logical steps in the innovation.

Jan Fagerberg, David Mowery, and Richard Nelson elucidate this innovative process: "Invention is the first occurrence of an idea for a new product or process, while innovation is the first attempt to carry it out in practice. Sometimes, invention and innovation are closely linked, to the extent that it is hard to distinguish one from the other. In most instances, however, there is a time lag between the two." [12]

This time lag is actually a benefit to organizations because it provides a chance to fully flesh out an idea, gather data to support its implementation, evaluate its potential for success, and make a determination as to the optimal time to launch the invention. The actual launching of the innovation is the work of change. Practice has demonstrated that innovation has its own time horizon, which is impacted by many variables. The key task for community college leaders is to determine the optimum time requirement needed to improve the likelihood for success of the innovation.

Austrian economist Joseph Schumpeter suggested that innovation is normally and institutionally experienced, particularly in larger organizations, in a variety of ways, including: 1) development of a new product, or a higher quality product; 2) introduction of a new methodology or process of production; 3) creation of a new market; 4) restructuring of an industry; and 5) through the application of new materials. [13]

Jospeh Schumpeter's pioneering work brought greater clarity to the construct of innovation, but it neglected the untidy process through which innovation unfolds, the unpredictable nature of process variables, and the effect of competing institutional priorities.

Innovation has its roots in creativity. Tony Davila, Marc Epstein, and Robert Shelton suggest that creativity promulgates ideas, whereas innovation transforms ideas into reality. They also note that a natural tension exists between creativity and innovation, but conclude that it is not a zero-sum relationship. [14] The process of innovation cannot exist apart from creativity; hence, institutional leaders must also be aware of organizational processes and culture, which can impede idea generation and stifle creativity.

Both change and innovation require significant work, sweat equity, the ability to endure failure and learn from it, and an organizational environment supportive of both. It is not for the faint of heart, nor the occasionally dedicated. As the common expression goes, "The world filters out the uncommitted."

THEORIES AND CONSTRUCTS OF CHANGE AND INNOVATION

As discussed earlier, the advancement and implementation of innovation and change are often difficult and may be thwarted by employees who resist them. Therefore, for the community college president to lead change at the institutional level to achieve particular objectives, he or she must first lead change at the personnel level. "The reality for organizations today is that employees have choice, capacity limitations and capability constraints. Change saturation is at an all-time high. Resistance to change from employees is the norm and not the exception, especially when change is being imposed by others. Failing to lead the people side of change results in lower utilization, slower speed of adoption and poorer proficiency."[15]

Hiatt and Creasy suggest change management as the core strategy for administrators to assist employees in understanding the institutional need for change, their role in it, establishment of a common language, and operational integration of the change for the long term. The authors believe that vital tools in the process include early involvement, communication, professional development, and coaching to build a common vision and commitment to the change effort.[16]

By understanding the particular mechanics of the change process, leaders can effectively advance needed change and obtain essential support, and incorporating a proven strategy for leading change and innovation is both prudent and instructive. Perhaps the most familiar and practical of organizational change theories was developed and presented by psychologist Kurt Lewin in 1948. His three-stage model is known as Unfreeze–Change–Refreeze, and is based upon an analogy of the changing shape of a block of ice.

The first stage of the process model is *unfreeze*, during which college leaders must communicate the "why" of the change, ensuring that everyone who will be affected by the change understands it. As part of this step, the college leadership must address employee doubts and concerns on a personal level.

The next step, *change*, represents the actual advancement of the change itself. At this juncture, employees become more familiar with the idea that things are moving to a different state. It is vital during this second step of the process that institutional leadership strongly supports employees, talking with them and reminding them of how the new initiative or innovation will advance the college mission and benefit the people involved. Doing so will encourage employees to continue to support the plan.

The final step in Lewin's model is *refreeze*. At this point, the intended change becomes part of the college's culture. As the institutional leader, your work is not done here. You must continue to ensure that employees have the ongoing support and professional development they need, which reinforces the change goal. Celebrating the goal achievement is also an important part of this step insofar as it brings closure to the process, and encourages employees to be more willing to engage in the next change process.[17]

Christensen (1997, 2000), Christensen and Raynor (2003) and Christensen and Eyring (2011) suggest that innovation occurs in two forms: *incremental or sustaining innovation* and *disruptive innovation*. Sustaining innovations represent the most modest of improvements to existing products and services through reduced cost, upgrades, increased speed, or streamlining, that is, producing better results by using what is currently available in the marketplace.[18]

These enhancements are designed to retain, and expand upon, the current customer base, growing revenues in the process. This form of innovation might be what we are defining as "change" in the broadest sense of the word, and it typifies the pattern of change in most organizations. These enrichments have limited utility in creating new markets for the organization.[19] In much the same vein, authors Jain, Triandis and Weick note that innovation can be either "incremental" or "radical," with each form characterized by the associated levels of risk and reward potential.[20]

To elucidate the differences between incremental or sustaining innovations and disruptive or radical innovations in community colleges, let's consider a few examples. A sustaining innovation could be manifested through the changing of class schedules and start times to make attendance more convenient for working students. As another example, colleges could adopt an "open entry/open exit" approach to classroom instruction, which would enable students to enter and exit classes on a flexible basis, as opposed to the traditional fifteen-week semester.

Alternatively, disruptive innovation moves beyond these minor tweaks to a level of organizational and operational change of significant magnitude, such as the creation of a new market niche or a new service strategy. For example, consider the introduction of Massive Open Online Courses (MOOCs). These large-scale, openly licensed, and generally tuition-free courses provide opportunities for instructors to distribute text, video, lecture notes, examinations, and other tools that allow students to take classes any time, any place, and at any pace.

Students can interact with thousands of students worldwide who are enrolled in the same class. While MOOCs have flaws, including a cumbersome delivery platform, unworkable financial sustainability, credit granting limits, and a low student success rate, they represent a dramatic change in the delivery of postsecondary education. They likewise represent a new market and a new service.

Early limitations, like those of MOOCs, display a unique characteristic of all disruptive innovations, and those limitations are the very reason why they are so dangerous to other marketplace competitors. Disruptive innovations of product and process initially appear on the edge of existing markets with little fanfare or notice. They tend to be clunky, awkward, and possess a number of operational flaws, making them inferior to those products and services currently available, so they are largely ignored by the current customer base—and therein lies their power.

Despite their limitations, the new disruptive innovations do appeal to new markets. Over time innovation is continuously improved, thereby drawing a larger customer base. By the time existing market competitors are aware of the new market entrant, or believe it to be a threat, it is likely too late to defend against it.

As an example, at the time of this writing, Arizona State University and edX announced the creation of the Global Freshman Academy (GFA). Through the GFA, students pay a nominal fee, avoid the messy business of admissions processing, and they may enroll in a full year of freshman-level, for-credit classes. Students who successfully complete the courses have the option of paying $200 per credit hour to have a course placed on their official transcript.[21]

Though the GFA credit hours are not yet eligible for Title IV aid, and details regarding the accreditation of the academy remain, it represents a continuing improvement of the MOOC innovation. MOOCs could grow in market appeal and acceptance and eventually surpass existing college credit- and degree-credentialing services. As with all disruptive innovations to higher education, community college leaders would be wise to consider how best to position themselves for, collaborate with, or otherwise adapt to this new innovation before it is too late.

Playing it safe and focusing only upon sustaining innovations is an unlikely pathway to long-term success. Through his research, Christensen identified numerous examples of organizations that ultimately failed because they followed the comfortable strategy of incremental improvement and a long-standing business model. In these cases, organizational leaders, shareholders, and stakeholders do not see a need for change, in part because they enjoy the bounty of the current model. Consequently, they fail to look ahead and anticipate market change, and they do not engage in the hard work of continuous innovation.

Borders Group, Inc., a bookstore company, founded in 1971 in Ann Arbor, Michigan, is an example of the aforementioned behavior. At the peak of its business, the company employed more than 19,000 people in 680 Borders stores, Waldenbooks stores, and other retail outlet stores nationwide. It also operated bookstores in Singapore, New Zealand, and Sydney. By most accounts, Borders was a successful company. However, in February 2011 the company filed for chapter 11 bankruptcy protection, and by September of that same year, Borders was gone. How could this happen?

Interestingly, Borders was a major player in the creation of the megastore business concept that others followed. The company was also an early developer of analytics that targeted, monitored, and leveraged customer purchasing patterns. However, deeply embedded in the Borders culture was strong commitment to their business model, massive investments in brick and mortar, and the trendy concept of patrons browsing through books, reading, conversing, and enjoying coffee and scones in comfortable facilities. So entrenched was this idea that the company didn't see the value in aggressively developing online sales and distribution channels, nor in promoting e-readers.

Borders invested more heavily in CDs and DVDs at a time when the industry was moving toward a digital platform, and they did not turn a profit beyond 2006. The company failed to check the horizon for disruptive innovations and innovators, and made only modest improvements to operations. Knowing that customers were interested in online purchases, yet believing that demand for online purchase would be limited over the long term, Borders outsourced its online work to Amazon, a company that was clearly focused on the changing horizon of this industry. For Borders, the desire to stay with the current business model was too strong to overcome—a desire that eventually led the organization to its demise.

Now, you may be musing that while these case examples are interesting, in the end they represent little more than the 20/20 vision of hindsight. Or you may believe that no organizational leader would knowingly drive his or her business into the ground with the prior knowledge that decisions made along the way would ultimately derail the institution, and you would be right on both counts. Indeed, this is the very purpose of this book: to examine those mental models, practices, behaviors, biases, and mistakes that lead to failure.

Maxwell Wessel and Clayton Christensen note that to some degree, we may be the victims of our own training and experience, which instruct us to focus not upon the value proposition we deliver to our customers, but rather upon proxies for it. A leader can point to visible, incremental improvements, like improving term-to-term persistence, as tangible evidence of moving the institution forward.

In this way, college leaders unwittingly spend more time competing for customers, commoditizing education, increasing dual enrollments, lowering prices, increasing revenues, and chasing things like reverse transfer credentialing, higher student persistence rates, and lower default rates[22]—all at the expense of disruptive innovation.

Wessel and Christensen urge that "before leaders engage in reckless price competition or squandering resources and effort in the futile defense of lost causes, they owe it to their employees and customers [students] to take stock of the entire situation and respond comprehensively, to meet disrupters with disruption of their own, but also to guide their legacy business toward as healthy a future as possible."[23]

Higher education leaders seem increasingly unable to discern the elements of the changing landscape before them. While some leaders may have experienced, and may even fundamentally believe, that modest improvements are sufficient to advance the institution toward key goals, failure to actively pursue and leverage the power of disruptive innovation is imprudent.

RISK, REWARD, CHANGE, ANXIETY AND THE WORKPLACE

John Kotter identifies global forces at play that are driving change in all organizations. Globalization of markets and competition, as well as advances in technology, he warns, are so vast that no organization is immune from their impact. These influences highlight the risk versus reward aspect of change.[24]

Absent a risk-reward calculation, a college could incorrectly conclude that a particular change has merit and should be deployed. For example, the reduction of building heating temperatures in the winter months, while on the surface a great idea for saving money, could prompt a decline in employee productivity and morale, as well as prompt a higher incidence of illness.

Likewise, a state legislature may conclude that introducing a new law is desirable, perhaps one requiring increased transparency reporting of community college activity, such as administrative costs, per-program costs, developmental education enrollments, student completion rates, transfer rates, job placement rates, and numerous other performance data. However, the increased research burden on the institution, especially for smaller colleges, in the absence of additional resource support, might require a transfer of funds from student support services to institutional research efforts, potentially diminishing the college's ability to provide essential assistance to students.

Figure 2.1 presents a logic model that contextualizes risk versus reward, as well as the duality of employee perceptions of change. In this model, change occurs along an x-y axis, upon which risk and the potential for reward are direct correlates. Change and the fear of change (i.e., level of anxiety) are correlates interacting with risk and reward.

A linear relationship exists between the type and magnitude of change intervention, the level of anxiety among those affected by change, and the potential for reward or propensity for risk. More specifically, as expressed along the y-axis, the more willing a leader is to embrace risk (i.e., the willingness to invest and lose something of value), the greater the potential of obtaining something of value.

The avoidance of risk (i.e., the act of doing nothing) is in itself a risk, leading to the all too familiar problems of vulnerability to competition, lack of growth, and in the extreme, organizational failure. With the initiation of a change activity, organizational stress grows, creating anxiety for employees. When a high-risk initiative is pursued, the level of organizational activity likewise rises, leading to a higher level of anxiety, which has its own set of challenges.

However, there is a negative effect when an opportunity is not pursued, and/or the magnitude of change is minimal. Negative effects typi-

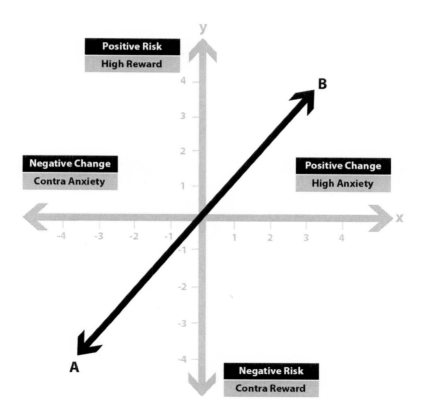

Figure 2.1. Change and Risk/Reward Relationships

cally manifest themselves as absence of motivation and innovation. "Positive change" in this model is a preferred state of being, while at the opposite end of the x-axis is "negative change," a state of decline or stasis.

Taken as a whole, this graphic demonstrates that as an intervention is undertaken, its placement on the A-B continuum will depend on four variables: risk, reward, nature of change, and anxiety level. Further, as the element of risk associated with the change increases, the potential reward increases as well, along with the level of personal anxiety. This duality also works in reverse. As risk and reward decrease, together with the level of personal anxiety, the effect of change will likewise decrease.

Of course, there are variants and exceptions to this model. Some change efforts may be both positive and negative. For example, some employees may embrace a new approach, while others may deplore it. Simple in design, this logic model provides a reference for the practical application of change and innovation as well as risk and reward in community colleges. It also provides a common language for change implementation among leaders and staff. Regardless of the model used, understanding essential relationships between risk, reward, change, and anxiety is central to understanding an organization's capacity for change.

BARRIERS TO CHANGE

No discussion of change would be complete without addressing attendant barriers to change and innovation in higher education, especially with the increased number of calls for improvement.

In November 2008, the Bill and Melinda Gates Foundation unveiled a goal to double, by 2025, the number of low-income students earning a postsecondary credential by the age of twenty-six. Likewise, President Obama declared in February 2009 that the number of graduates from colleges and universities must increase to a level that ranks the United States with having the highest proportion of college graduates worldwide by 2020.

The Lumina Foundation joined in this crusade, launching a "Big Goal" that 60 percent of Americans will have a higher education credential by 2025. The New American Foundation followed suit and decreed that by 2025, higher education must have a 50 percent increase in graduation rates. These statements of aspiration and demand are not hollow. They are a call to arms for higher education to remake itself, as achievement at these levels is not possible through incremental change.

In state governments as well, multiple forces are fueling these performance decrees. As National Center for Higher Education Management System (NCHEMS) leaders Dennis Jones and Patrick Kelly note, student outcomes are progressively and inextricably interwoven with how students and states pay for higher education, which is leading to protracted debates about higher education finance policy.

In many cases, states require higher education institutions to improve performance levels just to receive the same level of funding as they did in the past.[25] State support for community colleges is often tie-barred to performance metrics that include improvement in graduation rates, transfer rates, minority achievement rates, job placement rates, and administrative costs. Public community colleges in states like Ohio now have 100 percent of their state support tied to specific metrics and hurdle rates for student achievement.

So what is holding our community colleges and universities back from getting this achievement work done and meeting these goals? Daniel Rowley, Herman Lujan, and Michael Dolence identify barriers to achievement: "One inevitably must wrestle with a word that most academic faculty and administrators honestly do not like: change. Yet, as you look at the general issue of change in colleges and universities, it is important to observe that these intuitions change more slowly than other institutions and do not have a legacy of reacting happily or speedily to pressures to change. They are governed by traditions stretching back to the medieval days in European history."[26]

Referencing Robert Birnbaum's[27] work on academic senates, Rowley, Lujan, and Dolence further note:

> As Birnbaum suggests, those who would pursue change on the campus must be content with strong resistance, or inertia, which takes the form of laborious process and review and is at the core of campus politics in both faculty and administrative circles. Because reactiveness, as opposed to responsiveness, is the normal response of campus leaders, politics have been used to keep things from happening, from changing. The power of campus politics lies in a group's ability to veto change directly or surround it with procedure and ritual that confounds, dilutes, or smothers it. Unfortunately, the resulting inertia tends to be a typical response to external pressures for change, and, as a result, change seems to move at the proverbial snail's pace.[28]

Staunch resistance to institutional change combined with a resounding public mandate for change amounts to a perfect storm for higher education. Interestingly, long-standing universities and research institutions have responded, in part, by building a buffer between themselves and change. Distinguished histories, proud traditions, venerable names, scores of lobbyists, and influential alumni can provide insulation from the call to innovate. Community colleges, however, are not distinguished by history and tradition and, therefore, are not accorded the opportunity to avoid or delay the arrival of innovation.

A 2000 study by Laura Noone of forty-seven academic leaders confirmed the specific internal obstacles that contribute to the resistance of change. Noone reported, "As one leader put it, 'Inertia is a villain in the marketplace but is worshiped in higher education because we relish tradition.' Another respondent quipped 'The world has challenges but the college has departments. Most issues require integrative thinking that is interdisciplinary and our departments don't allow for that.'"[29]

Noone's study also revealed that a majority of academic leaders felt that their ability to innovate was "constrained" by institutional decision processes that were "substantial barriers." She found that academic freedom and the participatory governance structure of community colleges also presented a challenge to campus executives engaged in change.

These policies and practices result in an inequitable distribution of power, resources, and influence within institutions, all of which impacts senior managers' outlook on strategic decisions. She also noted that participatory governance fuels a culture of persuasion, negotiation, and consensus building. Therefore, college presidents are required to take on roles of conflict manager and facilitator of consensus—roles that increase the stakes and make it difficult to manage strategically while pandering to constituency expectations.[30]

Mary Locke and Lucy Guglielmino's study of college administrators' experience, and specifically the response of faculty to presidential initiatives, identifies employee concerns, including loss of authority, lack of transparency in the process, and inconvenient timing. Faculty perception of their value, as gleaned through consultation, contributed to their level of involvement in innovation initiatives.

Reactions from clerical staff were similar in that they appreciated inclusion and the value placed upon their input. Locke and Guglielmino note that in instances of successful change implementation, the decisions, communications, and actions of the institutional leader consistently acknowledged and addressed the beliefs and interests of campus constituencies.[31]

The findings of other researchers and scholars reaffirm the need for leaders to have a thoughtful and well-conceived plan, one that provides adequate communications and involves employees and constituent groups. A president might wrongly conclude that excluding faculty and staff from the planning and development process would accelerate the change process, owing to the absence of detractors. However, failing to involve and engage employees and other vital constituencies weakens the leader's position by sacrificing transparency and authenticity, the lack of which can derail the initiative.

By providing an opportunity for others to criticize the change initiative, the president may strengthen his or her hand by uncovering inherent weaknesses early in the plan's design with time to correct them. This is an important way to avoid the tendency for leaders to believe so strongly in their own vision for the future that they cannot see the flaws in it, or improvements that can be made.

INNOVATION OUTSIDE OF ACADEME

To understand innovation in the community college, it is helpful to understand the experience of organizations outside of higher education as well. According to John Bessant, the bulk of available research regarding innovation and change is derived from the private, for-profit sector. This research still has considerable application for public organizations.

He argues that "the issues are similar, and in many ways the public sector has had a great deal of experience in trying to deal with breakthrough innovations, which often change the rules of the game across the whole sector, or with managing the conflicting demands of multiple stakeholders. The difficulties of working within established frameworks, or risk aversion, of selection and resource allocation mechanisms which favor the status quo, are common to both sectors alike. There is similarly a strong need in both sectors to explore and experiment, trying to develop ways of managing effectively under these conditions."[32] Essays on change from a business perspective often, though less so recently, link success with a leader's characteristics, styles, and abilities.

> Education is seen as a matter of quality, and why should colleges or universities change their way of doing things? After all, it was higher education that made the United States first in the world of things and ideas, and is it not better to stay with the practices that created that quality and status in the first place? . . . [However], a fundamental change has occurred. Vast amounts of knowledge are rapidly becoming available to anyone connected to the extensive digital inter-linkages of the Internet and the World Wide Web. Colleges and universities are no longer the gatekeepers—they no longer hold the key to creating and disseminating information, let alone learning from it.[33]

It stands to reason then that higher education leaders should reach out to external organizations to better understand the views, philosophies, planning efforts, practical applications, and experiences of businesses in change and innovation practices. This may be somewhat difficult for higher education professionals to consider due to the fact that traditionally, the operational practices of businesses and the associated vernacular, let alone the approach to innovation, have not resonated with academe. Nevertheless, it is well past time to move beyond this limited, parochial thinking and to learn from others outside our realm, evaluate all available ideas, and incorporate them where feasible.

INCREMENTAL OR RADICAL INNOVATION?

It is well established that to succeed in the future, organizations must include change, disruptive innovation, and sustaining incremental innovation in their arsenal of strategies to remain competitive, as well as to thrive. It's also important to understand, as Clayton Christensen notes is his book, *The Innovator's Dilemma*, that technology is almost always involved.

As defined by Christensen and throughout this book, technology is defined as "the processes by which an organization transforms labor, capital, materials and information into products and services of greater value."[34] By this meaning, it is understood that all institutions have technologies. As in the case of higher education, technology could include delivery of instruction, development of contract training, or financial assistance through the college's foundation.

As an example, consider the plight of escalating textbook costs for students, which often results in using an increased share of the student's financial aid to offset the cost of textbooks. Consequently, students increasingly no longer use textbooks at all (by some accounts 30 percent of enrolled students never use a textbook). The opportunity to introduce a disruptively innovative approach is here.

The simple solutions are only incremental: limiting future edition changes, considering a textbook rental program, or binding select articles at Kinko's and calling it a textbook. True innovation could result from an understanding of how students learn, their sources and uses of information, and from changing processes and practices to accommodate their preferences.

In this case, disruptive innovation could occur through a "textbook-zero" environment. In this design, students bring their own digital technology (e.g., laptop, data pad, or phablet) to campus, or make a one-time purchase of a tablet from the college bookstore at a price roughly equivalent to a couple of textbooks. Faculty make full use of open educational resources (OERs) such as OpenStax, the Creative Commons, GNU General Public License, Academic Earth, MIT OpenCourseWare, OpenLearn and others.

Faculty essentially deliver the same quantity and quality of learning resources to students, with the added value of students having real-time access to rich, vibrant, and, in some cases, interactive content. This particular innovation has the added benefits of leveling the digital divide, often a challenge for community college students of diverse backgrounds, and enabling immediate access for group work in the flipped classroom, as well as a host of other applications.

A real-world example of this OER innovation currently is in place at Tidewater Community College (TCC) in Norfolk, Virginia. TCC partnered with Lumen Learning from Portland, Oregon, in 2013 to launch a two-year pilot of "Z-Degree," a textbook-free, OER-based program, and in so doing, became the nation's first community college to offer an associate of science degree completely through OERs.[35]

TCC was deeply concerned about the rising cost of textbooks for its students, which in 2015 was roughly $1,200 per year. So the college established and communicated a vision with two clear goals in addition to lowering student costs: 1) improve student outcomes, and 2) increase instructor effectiveness. TCC brought together a team of thirteen faculty members, who considered all options in collaboration with other administrators and staff, and forwarded the best ideas to administration as recommendations.

What resulted was a new approach to learning that involved professional development of instructors, course reconfiguration in a way that utilized OER materials to match required learning objectives, and delivery through the TCC's Blackboard course management system. When the work was completed, twenty-one "Z-Courses" from the Associate of Science in Business Administration program were made available at four TCC campus locations.

TCC, a college of some 47,000 students, believes that the Z-Degree program may save students about a quarter of the total cost of their degree program.[36] Though the jury is still out on the broad application of this innovation, feedback to date has been largely positive with 85 percent of Z-Degree students stating that they would choose another Z-Course over a traditional textbook-based course. This TCC project demonstrates the potential for success when vision, research, communication, preparation, involvement, and execution of innovation are effectively combined.

In a similar vein, the University of Wisconsin (UW), after examining the unique needs of its nontraditional students, developed a new "tuition subscription model" entitled the "UW Flexible Option." Launched in 2013, the competency-based education program provides a pathway to degree completion by giving students credit for knowledge gained prior to enrollment, and allowing them to advance through the material at their own pace without the traditional fifteen-week semester.

Students begin and end when it makes sense for them to do so, based upon their own personal circumstances. The majority of the coursework and support materials is available online. Tuition is structured around two models: an "All-You-Can-Learn" option, essentially a three-month enrollment period in which students can enroll for as many classes as they wish for the fixed price of $2,250; and a "Single Competency Set" option, also for a three-month period, which costs $900.

Enrollment subscription periods begin the second day of each month. Supporting UW students in this new learning design is an academic success coach from the college, who is with the student every step of the way through graduation. At the end of the program, students hold a competency-based degree that is of interest and value to employers.[37]

Both the TCC "Z-Degree Program" and the UW "Flexible Option Program" disrupt the traditional approach to the delivery of education. In addition to the obvious changes and associated benefits to students, these initiatives also disrupt the operational model of higher education.

To be sure, it is cumbersome for colleges to obtain federal waivers and adjust their financial aid options to accommodate competency-based education, to say nothing of the complications involved for registrars in transferring these credits, and faculty who struggle to determine what letter grade to apply to the accumulation of competencies.

The revenue side of the institutional ledger, usually supplemented significantly by textbook and credit hour sales, is also disrupted. The UW tuition model is untidy insofar as college business officers cannot determine the exact amount of revenue or expense involved because they cannot accurately predict how many credit hours a student may take in a three-month period. I suspect that because institutional leaders cannot justify the lost revenue, especially when trying to determine how those revenues might be restored through other sources, the aforementioned programs have not been universally well received.

Finally, consider how community college and university faculty are required to redesign courses for use in the new formats for both of these initiatives. To the degree that we can judge innovation by the extent of teamwork and adjustment necessary, it is easy to see why new delivery systems are disruptive. Over time, I believe that these types of innovations will more than likely become the dominant model of higher education delivery, much to the chagrin of faculty and staff who do not envision a future shaped by disruptive change.

THE PARADOX OF INNOVATION

The broad pursuit of disruptive innovation seems like an obvious solution for what ails business and higher education alike. However, working against the acceptance of disruptive innovation is research that identifies numerous organizations that ultimately failed with innovation efforts because leaders merely improved the current model (i.e., engaged in sustaining innovation) while ignoring new, unconventional, breakthrough innovative systems, processes, practices, and the environment,[38] just like Borders did.

However, the opposite can also be true, which is to say organizations can become so focused on pursuing disruptive innovations that they forgo obvious incremental opportunities to grow revenues and build market position through better operations and efficiencies.[39] Innovation is not a zero-sum game. That's the innovation paradox.

As an example among community colleges, those institutions that have been slow to adopt or have ignored innovations such as online education, have experienced a drop in enrollment as students have migrated to online institutions.[40] However, those institutions that have invested significant resources in online education could be losing students, their long-term loyalty, and associated revenues, by not improving personalized education, an important component for students who need extra support.

The innovation paradox is not a new phenomenon. There have been many articles over the past twenty-five years that have noted the important differences between sustaining innovation and disruptive innovation. However, there has not been a clear consensus as to whether certain types of organizations lend themselves better to innovation work.

Researcher Wendy Smith suggests that "incremental and radical innovations are associated with seemingly competing goals and inconsistent architectures, structures, cultures, processes, and leadership profiles. Innovating involves experimenting, failing, and learning, and it is best supported by flat organizational structures with an entrepreneurial culture. In contrast, incrementally improving the existing product involves efficiency and optimization, and it is best supported by hierarchical organizational structures and bureaucratic cultures."[41]

To better evaluate the more significant, and perhaps institutionally resonating differences, Mark Rice, Gina O'Connor, Lois Peters, and Joseph Morone provide a model for evaluating core differences between sustaining innovation and disruptive innovation (as shown in figure 2.2) across eight distinctive characteristics.[42]

Characteristic	Sustaining	Disruptive
Timeframe/Duration	Short term (weeks or months)	Long term (multiple years)
Predictability of outcome	Some certainty	Highly uncertain
Rate of progress	Steady	Sporadic with many stops and starts
Process	Methodical and sequential	Highly non-linear
Framework	Context-independent	Context-dependent
Paradigm	Mechanistic and targeted	Organic and experimental
Variables	Limited number and small range	Stochastic
Scope	Mainly internal; contained	Exogenous events are critical

Figure 2.2. Implementation Characteristics for Sustaining versus Disruptive Innovations

This matrix examines the type of innovation under consideration, as well as implications for the institution considering it. Taken as a whole, the limited research that is available for community colleges indicates that institutions are unique, but they have two characteristics in common when it comes to innovation: 1) there are cultural, political, and structural barriers that stand in the way of innovation in all organizations, and 2) leaders must have skills, inclination, and board support to advance the college through the tumult of disruptive innovation. It suggests that the success of sustaining and disruptive innovation is largely contingent upon the abilities of the leader, as well as his or her proclivities toward change.

LEADERSHIP AND THE CHALLENGE OF CHANGE

Leaders must balance operational pressures from myriad internal and external forces. Derek Bok notes that "the most promising innovations can languish unless some effective force causes them to be emulated widely,"[43] which suggests that the sustainability of initiatives depends, in large part, on the skills of leaders.

In the same vein, Neal Gross, Joseph Giacquinta, and Marilyn Berstein as well as Kevin Quinlan identify the organizational leader as principally and ultimately responsible for the success or failure of innovation.[44] No matter how alluring an innovation might be, it is dead in the water without a leader, and a capable leadership team. Leaders must concurrently perform multiple roles: managing day-to-day operations, interacting with various publics, coaching, working with trustees, visioning, communicating, managing budgets, raising funds, talking with students, and mediating the needs of internal staff while simultaneously promoting innovation. Indeed, the conflicting needs of all stakeholders have the potential to compound and distract from advancing innovation.

Steve Denning summarizes the challenge facing organizational leaders and decision makers, noting that "managers succumb to pressures to run away from disruptive innovation rather than stand and fight because [innovations] represent a threat to management, to careers, to power structures, to customary ways of doing things, to client bases, to brands, and to corporate culture."

Decision making is conservative; it reflects a fear of disruption of entrenched power structures and careers. "In fact . . . managers usually have the most to lose in any basic change so they're likely to devote their resources to innovations that bolster current fiefdoms and careers and against disruptive innovation."[45] Although Denning is referring to managers of organizations in general, his observations are also ensconced in the culture of community colleges. Strategic and supportive leadership is not the sole ingredient for effective change management in community colleges, but it is, without question, an essential component for successful change and innovation.

DEMYSTIFYING CHANGE

The forms and dimensions of change and innovation are complex and their implementation challenges even the best of leaders. Redirecting the community college toward innovation for strategic advantage and improved service involves risk, but also the potential for intrinsic rewards.

Change is neither static nor finite. Change is not linear. Change is organic, and as such it has no predictable pattern and has no boundaries. Its implications are for the most part continuous. Adding to the difficulty in planning and implementing change are threats and opportunities that are not easily observed or readily understood. The president does not have a universal guide to timing nor the perfect knowledge of conditions under which he or she should pursue an innovation or choose to let others work first on the bleeding edge. Add to this the harsh reality that community college cultures are often risk-averse and inhabited by faculty and staff who view change as troublesome and unnecessary, at best. Taken together, this is a maelstrom for the perfect storm.

Practically speaking, however, we know that environmental and competitive realities make change unavoidable. Institutions are best served by leaders and staff who understand change and are prepared to lead it rather than simply react to it. Leaders need to engage external organizations in the process through open and forthright research, observation, and dialogue about intentions, goals, risks, and desired outcomes. Part of the solution involves helping personnel become comfortable with change and reducing the message to understandable, manageable chunks and standing by commitments.

Theories, ideas, constructs, and mental models abound with regard to change and innovation, the preponderance of which exists within business and industrial organizations. Scholarly literature and published research from a variety of disciplines offer frameworks for understanding change and innovation, and their paradoxical nature. I strongly recommend that institutional leaders, rather than subscribing to a single model, draw from research and the experience of others to find an innovation model to best meet their needs, guided by a clear understanding of the strengths and limitations of their own organization. In chapter 3, I provide such a model for consideration.

NOTES

1. Juett R. Cooper, "A Multidimensional Approach to the Adoption of Innovation," *Management Decision* 36, 8 (1998): 493–502.
2. Tara Kulash, "25 Percent Do Not Change Bad Health Habits after Heart Attack, Stroke." *St. Louis Post Dispatch*, August 15, 2013. Accessed September 12, 2014. http://www.stltoday.com/lifestyles/health-med-fit/percent-do-not-change-bad-health-habits-after-heart-attack/article_f30164af-2368-5cf5-8bdc-3f641a7607b8.html.

3. Tandi M. Hartle, "Disease Ridden Patients Refuse to Make Lifestyle Changes." *Natural News* (May 31, 2011). Accessed July 21, 2014. http://www.naturalnews.com/032561_lifestyle_changes_patients.html#.

4. Jeffery M. Hiatt and Timothy J. Creasy, *Change Management: The People Side of Change* (Loveland, CO: Prosci, Inc., 2012), 1.

5. Hiatt and Creasy, *Change Management: The People Side of Change*, 10.

6. Marshal S. Poole and Andrew H. Van de Ven, eds., *Handbook of Organizational Change and Innovation* (New York: Oxford University Press, 2004).

7. Stephen P. Osborne and Kerry Brown, *Managing Change and Innovation in Public Service Organizations* (New York: Routledge, 2005), 4.

8. Jeff DeGraff and Shawn Quinn, *Leading Innovation: How to Jump Start Your Organization's Growth Engine* (New York: McGraw-Hill Companies, Inc., 2007), 8.

9. Jeff Osborne and Shawn Brown, *Managing Change and Innovation in Public Service Organizations*, 4.

10. DeGraff and Quinn, Leading Innovation: *How to Jump Start Your Organization's Growth Engine*, 8.

11. League for Innovation in the Community College, *The Nature of Innovation in the Community College* (Phoenix, AZ: Author, 2010), 5.

12. Jan Fagerberg, David C. Mowery, and Richard R. Nelson, eds., *The Oxford Handbook of Innovation* (New York: Oxford University Press, 2005), 4–5.

13. Joseph A. Schumpeter, *The Theory of Economic Development* (Cambridge, MA: Harvard University Press, 1934).

14. Tony Davila, Marc J. Epstein, and Robert D. Shelton, *Making Innovation Work: How to Manage It, Measure It, and Profit from It* (Upper Saddle River, NJ: Pearson Education, 2006).

15. Hiatt and Creasy, *Change Management: The People Side of Change*, 7.

16. Ibid.

17. Morten Levin, "Organizational Innovation Is a Participative Process," in *A Companion to Organizational Anthropology*, Douglas D. Caulkins and Ann T. Jordan, eds. (Chichester, West Sussex, UK: Blackwell Publishing, Ltd., 2013).

18. Clayton M. Christensen, *The Innovator's Dilemma* (Cambridge, MA: Harvard Business School Press, 1997); Clayton M. Christensen, "Assessing Your Organization's Innovation Capabilities." *Leader to Leader* (Summer 2001): 27–37; Clayton M. Christensen and Michael E. Raynor, *The Innovator's Solution* (Cambridge, MA: Harvard Business School Press, 2003); Clayton M. Christensen and Henry J. Eyring, *The Innovative University: Changing the DNA of Higher Education From the Inside Out* (San Francisco, CA: Jossey Bass, 2011).

19. Clayton M. Christensen, *The Innovator's Dilemma: the Revolutionary National Bestseller That Changed the Way We Do Business*. Rev. and updated ed. (New York: HarperBusiness, 2000).

20. Ravi K. Jain, Harry C. Triandis, and Cynthia Wagner Weick, *Managing Research, Development, and Innovation: Managing the Unmanageable*, 3rd ed. (Hoboken, NJ: John Wiley & Sons, Inc., 2010).

21. Charles Huckabee, "Arizona State and edX Will Offer an Online Freshman Year, Open to All," *Chronicle of Higher Education* (April 23, 2015). Accessed on April 26, 2015. http://chronicle.com/blogs/ticker/arizona-state-and-edx-will-offer-an-online-freshman-year-open-to-all/97685.

22. Maxwell Wessel and Clayton M. Christensen, "Surviving Disruption," *Harvard Business Review* (December 2012): 56–64.

23. Ibid, 64.

24. John P. Kotter, *Leading Change* (Boston: Harvard Business School Press, 1996).

25. Patrick J. Kelly and Dennis P. Jones, *A New Look at the Institutional Component of Higher Education Finance: A Guide for Evaluating Performance Relative to Financial Resources* (Boulder, CO: Author, 2007).

26. Daniel J. Rowley, Herman D. Lujan, and Michael G. Dolence, *Strategic Change in Colleges and Universities: Planning to Survive and Prosper*. San Francisco: Jossey-Bass Publishers, 1997, 7.

27. Robert Birnbaum, "The Latent Organizational Functions of the Academic Senate: Why Senates Do Not Work But Will Not Go Away." In *Faculty in Governance: The Role of Senates and Joint Committees in Academic Decision Making*, vol. 19, no. 3 *New Directions for Higher Education*, ed. Robert Birnbaum, no. 75 (Fall 1989): 7–25.

28. Rowley, Lujan, and Dolence, *Strategic Change in Colleges and Universities: Planning to Survive and Prosper*, 7.

29. Laura P. Noone, "Perceived Barriers to Innovation: First Report from a Study on Innovation in Higher Education." *Assessment and Accountability Forum* (Summer 2000), 1–7, in Otto W. K. Lee, "The Innovator's Dilemma and the Experience of Community College Leaders: A Phenomenological Inquiry" (Ph.D. diss., Fielding Graduate University, 2009).

30. Ibid.

31. Mary G. Locke and Lucy Guglielmino, "The Influence of Subcultures on Planned Change in a Community College." *Community College Review* 34, no. 2 (2006): 108–127, in Otto W. K. Lee, "The Innovator's Dilemma and the Experience of Community College Leaders: A Phenomenological Inquiry" (Ph.D. diss., Fielding Graduate University, 2009).

32. John Bessant, "Enabling Continuous and Discontinuous Innovation: Learning from the Private Sector," *Public Money & Management* 25 (January 2005), 35–42.

33. Rowley, Lujan, and Dolence, *Strategic Change in Colleges and Universities: Planning to Survive and Prosper*, 22–23.

34. Clayton M. Christensen, *The Innovator's Dilemma: When New Technologies Cause Great Firms to Fail* (Boston, MA: Harvard Business School Press, 1997), xvi.

35. Tidewater Community College, "Tidewater Community College Partners with Lumen Learning to Offer Textbook-Free Degree." Accessed November 1, 2014. http://www.tcc.edu/news/press/2013/TextbookFreeDegree.htm.

36. Ibid.

37. University of Wisconsin System "UW Flexible Option." Accessed March 1, 2015. http://flex.wisconsin.edu.

38. Clayton M. Christensen, *The Innovator's Dilemma: When New Technologies Cause Great Firms to Fail*.

39. Tony Davila and Marc J. Epstein, *The Innovation Paradox: Why Good Businesses Kill Breakthroughs and How They Can Change* (San Francisco, CA: Berrett-Koehler Publishers, Inc., 2014), 2.

40. National Council on Educational Statistics. *Distance Education at Degree-Granting Postsecondary Intuitions: 2006-07*. (2008). Accessed November 1, 2014. http://nces.ed.gov/pubs2009/2009044.pdf.

41. Wendy K. Smith, "Managing Strategic Contradictions: Top Management Teams Balancing Existing Products and Innovation Simultaneously" (Unpublished Dissertation, Harvard University, Cambridge, 2006), in Otto W. K. Lee, "The Innovator's Dilemma and the Experience of Community College Leaders: A Phenomenological Inquiry" (Ph.D. diss., Fielding Graduate University, 2009).

42. Mark P. Rice et al., "Managing Discontinuous Innovation," in *Research Technology Management* 41, no. 3 (1998): 52–58.

43. Derek Bok, *Higher Learning* (Cambridge, MA: Harvard University Press, 1986), 176.

44. Neal Gross, Joseph B. Giacquinta, and Marilyn Berstein, *Implementing Organizational Innovations*. New York: Basic Books, 1971; and Kevin P. Quinlan, "Chief Executive Officers in Atlantic Canada's Community Colleges: How Environment and Stakeholders Shape the Role" (Unpublished Dissertation, University of Toronto, Toronto 1995), in Otto W. K. Lee, "The Innovator's Dilemma and the Experience of Community College Leaders: A Phenomenological Inquiry" (Ph.D. diss., Fielding Graduate University, 2009).

45. Steve Denning, "Why the Best and Brightest Approaches Don't Solve the Innovation Dilemma." *Strategy & Leadership,* 33, no. 1 (2005): 5–6, in Otto W. K. Lee, "The Innovator's Dilemma and the Experience of Community College Leaders: A Phenomenological Inquiry" (Ph.D. diss., Fielding Graduate University, 2009).

THREE

Change and Innovation: Preparing the Institution for Success

"Progress is a nice word. But change is its motivator. And change has its enemies."
—Robert Kennedy

Institutional inertia is a powerful and prevailing force, and it abhors change. The introduction of even the slightest operational deviation encounters opposition urging a return to the prior course and speed of the organization. This inertia is often fueled by long-standing academic tradition, institutional structures, mores, political realities, staff resistance, and fear.

Should a "change agent" choose to pursue a new objective or initiative, he or she will most assuredly meet a counterforce to return to the former state, seemingly in accordance with Newton's third law of motion (for every action, there is an opposite and equal reaction). These dynamisms may present themselves as peer pressure, disassociation, or even subterfuge.

Even if a leader can surmount these opposing forces, he or she still must face the practical realties of obtaining budget support, building communications strategies, determining project timing, and perhaps even encountering failure. Given these and many other related trials, it's no surprise that the status quo can look pretty enticing.

Knowing that change waits for no one, as leaders we make the intentional decision to pursue it as a success strategy for our colleges, full in the knowledge that it will require the aforementioned work, and more. In so doing, we must acknowledge on the front end that this work can be untidy, uncomfortable, and even the source of our undoing.

As noted by Maxwell Wessel and Clayton Christensen, "[d]isruption is less a single event than a process that plays out over time, sometimes quickly and completely, but other times slowly and incompletely."[1] Institutional leaders must be mindful that there can be no assumptions when it comes to change. Serendipity doesn't work either. Furthermore, no leader can simply will a successful and sustainable innovation into reality through position, power, and edict, righteous in the belief that it is the right thing to do.

As Clayton Christensen and Henry Eyring remind us, "a common mistake made by many [leaders] is to assume that by building awareness of the need for change, they have also created a desire among employees to engage in that change. The assumption is that one automatically follows the other. Some [leaders] fall into the trap: If I design a 'really good' solution to a business problem, my employees will naturally embrace that solution. Resistance from employees takes these managers by surprise and they find themselves unprepared to manage that resistance."[2]

I have found in my own experience that employee support cannot be assumed no matter how visionary the leader or how innovative the idea. Why? First, because no matter how inspired or inspiring the proposed initiative, change is generally perceived as a loss by employees. It's often confusing, destabilizing, disorienting, and decidedly unwelcome. And second, because you are viewed by employees as "the disrupter." It is you who is bringing forward the change and thereby disrupting things.

This is true, in part, because you advocate for the change and cannot divorce yourself from the proposal in which you are invested. And it's also true because you are the institutional leader. Ergo, *you* become the issue. Some in your employ will hope to wait you out until you move on in your career. True innovation and change can only be realized through people, particularly in a human-resource-rich environment like higher education, and to attain the desired goals, people must be invested in the proposed work and have trust in those who are advancing it.

For example, assume that I have just returned from the latest American Association of Community Colleges' Annual Convention, having heard of the benefits of, say, a particular software for a course management system (CMS) that would improve our college's ability to administer, track, report, and deliver educational technology. No matter how much our employees may dislike the current software provider, no matter how impressed I was at the convention, no matter how much money the college will save, no matter how much their reporting tools are exactly what we need to make better decisions about our distance learning efforts, I can make no assumptions about the willingness of our faculty and staff to accept a change in the CMS.

I can come back filled with enthusiasm and excitement about the new product; however, they did not experience what I experienced. They did not hear what I heard. They may not be clear about the nature of the problems with the current system, and they are very busy people. If I attempt to push this agenda without the proper understanding of what is required in the associated change process, without the necessary relationships, without the involvement of others or a process plan, there will be issues aplenty.

For one thing, staff will be worried every time I head off to a conference. For another, the label "disrupter president" is not a good moniker for the long term. Consequently, it is imperative to change the narrative and the approach.

In order to move through a proposed change while retaining the respect of your employees and their willingness to continue to work with you to advance the day-to-day business of the college and whatever other promising innovation will come next, you might consider putting something or someone else between you and the innovation. Bring forward external, secondary data that show the higher success rates for your proposed innovation. Perhaps you contract with consultants to work with your faculty and IT staff to outline the benefits of a new CMS, based upon employee input and an assessment of current operations. Or perhaps you send teams of faculty and staff to benchmark against peer institutions. Regardless of method, creating space between the leader and the change is an advisable strategy.

The question now becomes this: With so many opposing forces, challenges, and sensitivities, is it possible to prepare for, pursue, and succeed with innovation and change? Is it possible to increase the likelihood of success? If so, is there an optimum approach for gathering, scaffolding, and deploying the core components of innovation (i.e., leadership preparation, institutional preparation, assessment and planning, and execution and evaluation) without the institutional leader being cast overboard?

I believe that the answer is "yes" and, indeed, this affirmation is the basis for this book. It is advisable for leaders to have a solid, clear approach to advance creativity, change, and innovation through inquiry and by constantly assessing the landscape, planning, and engaging employees, ultimately moving the institution toward enhanced relevance. Let's consider a few contemporary strategies and examples.

MODELS FOR CHANGE AND INNOVATION

Jeff Degraff and Shawn Quinn suggest, after twenty years of applied research, that the foremost problem in advancing innovation is the cumbersome nature of current processes and systems, even those that are specifically created to support change and innovation. Rather, the authors believe that innovation is the byproduct of numerous organizational experiences, experiments, and other activities that happen every day through many engaged employees.

To better define and guide others to work in this practicality, they developed the theory for leading innovation in organizations. The approach incorporates seven steps (as shown in figure 3.1) that may be used in whole or in part, concurrently or sequentially.

The method's design and sequence begins with the Synthesize function, which involves assessing and diagnosing an organization's purposes (outcomes), practices (i.e., capabilities, organizational culture, and competencies), and people (i.e., individual employees who create capabilities, culture, and competencies). Step two: strategize. Create a vision for the future and a road map that leads to it. Socialize, the third step, establishes a shared vision and values within the leadership team. Step four, Supervise, develops facilitators to lead and sustain change and innovation. Step five is Synchronize. Engage leaders throughout the organization to operationalize change. Next is Specialize, which seeks to jumpstart change and innovation action teams. Finally, Systemize reviews and revises projects, and adjusts organizational practices and learning.[3]

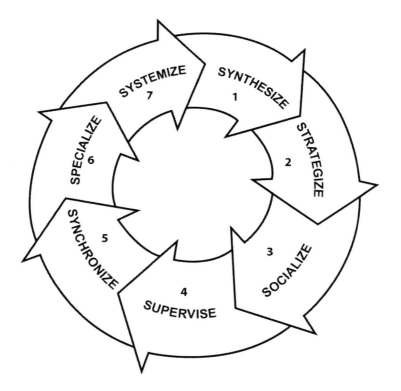

Figure 3.1.   The Creativize Model

Through this method, the authors explain that organizational innovation is a decidedly normal function, nothing special, and that, in fact, it explains why and how the institution can continue. Long-term growth is simply a matter of codifying, amplifying, and sustaining these actions.

Considering another model, one more particular to higher education, authors Rowley and Sherman, in their book *From Strategy to Change: Implementing the Plan in Higher Education*, consider a number of actions, some running concurrently, others separately. Based upon their research, they determine that there are essentially eleven methods for implementing strategic change in colleges, which are

- Using the budget to fund strategic change;
- Using participation;
- Using force;
- Establishing goals and key performance indicators;
- Working within the human resource management system of the campus to plan for and create change;
- Using the reward system to foster and support change;
- Working with or moving away from tradition;
- Developing and using changed champions; and
- Building on systems that are ready for, or are easily adaptable to, strategic change.

The two authors further note that a campus leader could use one, many, or all of these methods, depending on the college environment, resistance, culture, or leader skill sets. They also note that all but the last three methods produce a quicker outcome, while the remaining three are more long-term strategies.[4]

Still others believe in following specific sets of steps end-to-end, in order to reduce risk. Marriott School of Management authors Nathan Furr and Jeffrey Dyer are just such believers. Following many years of observation in industry, they have concluded that companies that succeed with innovation and change have followed four sequential steps: 1) Generate Insights—be attentive to persistent issues that may be worth further investigation through direct observation, networks, and research; 2) Identify an Important Problem—codify a problem from these observations that has yet to be solved and that if resolved could be a viable proposition for the organization; 3) Develop the Solution—experiment with various ideas and then test them with targeted consumers to determine acceptance levels, ultimately approving the strongest candidate; and lastly 4) Devise the Business Model—devise an appropriate and sustainable financial, promotional, distributional, and operational model to support the innovation. Deviation from any of these steps, argue the authors, will lead to suboptimal outcomes.[5]

Furr and Dyer cite the experience of Kraft General Foods as an example of an initiative that failed initially. When Kraft opened in the Chinese market in 1984, it did not announce a bold new vision for China, or push boundaries through seeking an understanding of its new environment (i.e., Generate Insights). By 2006, revenues from its product line were still sluggish and the company was losing money. It subsequently launched a "blank check initiative" that involved sending three senior leaders to China and giving them one year to assess things and make changes as needed.

The trio observed the customer base and held numerous focus groups to better understand the Chinese people and, more importantly, to ascertain the company's problems. As a result of their consumer questioning and consideration of other business models, they decided to move away from their traditional Oreo Cookies.

They experimented with multiple prototypes of Oreos: square ones, less filling, multiple layers, and many new flavors. They identified the best solution candidates and built a business model around these changes. Eventually, Kraft witnessed a six-fold increase in revenues with Oreos shaped like drinking straws, Green Tea Ice Cream Oreos, and Peanut Butter Oreos.[6] Only when the company dared to move beyond the status quo, engaged their employees, aggressively pursued new ideas, and took risks did they succeed with innovation.

Another interesting approach to advancing innovation is advanced by Michael Tushman who is both a director of Change Logic, LLC, and professor of business administration and chair of the Program for Leadership and Development at Harvard University. He suggests that the organizational leader become a Janus of sorts (the god of beginnings and transitions, according to ancient Roman mythology, often depicted as having two faces, since he looks to the future and to the past).

In a similar way, Tushman suggests that the leader approach innovation in both reactive and proactive terms. He defines this as organizational ambidexterity: "the ability of an organization to explore and exploit; to compete with mature technologies and in mature markets where efficiency, control and incremental improvements are prized; and to compete with new technologies in new markets where flexibility, autonomy and experimentation are preferred."[7]

This paradox, according to Tushman, is central to institutional sustainability because it leverages current revenue streams, while also risking by exploring new innovations, and managing the natural tension that occurs between them, such as competition for resources.

He notes four warning signs that, if observed, are a clear indication that organizational problems are in the offing and the leader should adopt an ambidextrous view. These include: 1) *short-term thinking* — favoring quick impact and solid results; 2) *investing more in exploitation than exploration* — an unbalanced organization given to cutting back on innovation when times get tough; 3) *from alignment to inertia* — living on the glory of current success rather than monitoring the changing environment; and

4) *the age of senior teams* —leadership groups who have worked together so long that they begin thinking alike and losing their edge.[8] Each of these warning signs includes both a present and future context, suggesting a dual responsibility in leading innovation.

Tushman's view is particularly insightful from a contemporary and rule-of-thumb manner of operating. His second warning, Investing More in Exploitation than Exploration, I find particularly on point and have seen the effects of it many times over. For example, when finances become stressed, and budgets need to be pared, most often colleges choose to eat their seed corn.

This farming metaphor, from my early days growing up in the tall grass prairie region of Iowa, suggests limited thinking and a poor decision point for the future and for long-term growth. Even in the poorest of times, farmers would not choose to eat the seed corn that they need to plant in the following spring. They would make other choices. Often in lean times, colleges choose to eliminate professional development, travel, marketing, and the like, when perhaps they should be doing precisely the opposite. To be a leader of change and innovation means to question our traditional thinking and practices and dare to define ourselves anew.

AN ARCHETYPE FOR CHANGE AND INNOVATION

Following the previous discussions of various constructs of change, multiple related theories regarding its effects upon people, implementation strategies, discussions, and examples, I'm sure that you've come to the same conclusion regarding the advancement of change and innovation as I have.

Essentially, the organizational leader must first appreciate the multidimensional complexity of change and innovation. Furthermore, given their organic and sometimes ineffable nature, I believe that change and innovation resist confinement to any one philosophy. Even the most balanced theoretical combinations, modality designs, and collaborations are not guarantees of success. There are just too many variables.

The differences between and among community colleges —their history, culture, employees, boards, institutional cohesion, charters, labor contracts, and local economy—all, in some way or fashion, undercut widely applicable theories. If a leader can accept these facts and understand the capricious dynamism of change, then it is possible to reduce the process into its broad components and develop a reasonable, replicable strategy for success that is unique to an institution.

As an example of the importance of acknowledging and addressing institutional differences, I offer the following personal anecdote. I arrived on the central campus of Jackson Community College (now Jackson College) in early 2001 as the new president. After a few years, I concluded from research, experience, and many conversations with area school superintendents, students, counselors, and parents, that there was a viable, yet unmet need at the college: student housing.

I learned that a sizable number of students were not considering attending our fine college because they wanted a "complete college experience," which included the opportunity for residence life. At that time, only a handful of Michigan's twenty-eight community colleges had dorms. When we further researched each of the institutions that did, we found that most of the colleges' staff complained of housing-related problems such as alcohol abuse, drug use, noise, physical altercations, personal violations, late bill payments, and the destruction of college property.

For some of the colleges, the issues were so bothersome that they said they wished they didn't have housing. Still, having worked in other states wherein many of the community colleges offered housing, having introduced and developed housing on other campuses, and even having served as a housing director and resident assistant (RA) in the past, I felt that with support, we could move the initiative forward to a positive outcome.

After exploring the idea of housing with our staff for a year, and still confident in the idea, I resolved to introduce it to the college's board of trustees at a semiannual planning session. Based upon research, I spoke of the need to meet student demand, the changing community college landscape, the self-liquidating loan-repayment strategy from monthly rental charges, sustainable building designs, the competitive advantage it would create, and the positive implications of housing upon student retention.

In turn, they expressed little to no interest overall, and felt the timing was not right. I was dumbfounded because the data were obvious, and I had approached the issue in much the same way with other community college boards in the past and received a favorable response.

I asked what more the board needed to be convinced, and they asked for more information. At the next planning session we presented data from other states and supportive articles and examples of other housing projects built on community college campuses, but to no avail. The majority of the trustees remained unsupportive, and they still felt that the time was not right.

This time, they asked for additional information on student demand, best practices, and costs. At this stage, we undertook yet another external survey of area students, and I also took it upon myself to speak to the president of a neighboring private, four-year college about the idea, suggesting a possible collaboration. Our college could host students for two years, and upon completion of their associate degree, interested students could transfer to his institution for their baccalaureate degree and live in their housing. My colleague didn't like this idea either. He didn't believe that housing was appropriate for community colleges (I should have picked up on this clue of regional differences).

At the next board planning session, we brought in a survey consultant and provided feedback from advisory groups, but the board's interest hovered at tepid. For the third time, we were asked to seek out more demand data, survey trends, and information on the experiences of our peers, which we did. At the succeeding board planning session, we had an even more definitive confirmation of demand, another consultant who offered the same conclusions, and an architect with project designs, renderings, and probable cost calculations. This time, we were authorized to proceed—three years later. Hallelujah!

In considering this process in retrospect, I see that besides modest additions of entirely new information at each planning session, the general idea, the purpose, the scope of the proposal, and the cost projections remained essentially the same. What made the difference? Well, perhaps we just wore them down, but it's more likely that I was experiencing how each community college board is different, and my approach needed to be adjusted accordingly.

More practically still, this board required more time to consider two things in order to support this significant change: 1) I was still an unproven leader in my brief tenure at the college, and housing represented a significant risk to them. They needed to better understand me as their president—my thinking process, the level of my commitment and resolve to deliver a successful project, my experience, my approach to planning, implementation, and contingencies; and 2) timing.

I kept hearing one particular trustee say, "It's just not the right time." I really didn't understand at first what she meant. Later I came to learn that she was reflecting that the board needed time to get comfortable with change, something that had not been pursued at the college for a number of years. The redundant review of data and information over time, while helpful, actually gave them more of what they really needed: time to consider change.

Recall that this board had never had housing on campus, though they had heard horror stories from their peers, and they knew it was a financial risk. I believe that we garnered confidence together—slowly—through an attention to detail, and by diffusing potential causes of risk and failure. Over time, trust grew and they could not ignore the proposed benefits to our students and the community. They opted to take the risk.

I suspect that if you were to ask any one of them today, they would tell you that we should have undertaken the initiative much earlier, and expanded the project scope, but it takes time to build this level of confidence. By the fall of 2015, the college opened its third student housing unit to an additional two hundred residential students who, according to the data, likely would have chosen another college if not for our housing.

Today at our college, even having realized success with this one initiative, we know all too well that we must constantly cultivate and support a positive institutional culture regarding change if we are to successfully move the next initiative forward and remain competitive.

In the business of innovation and change, you do not have the luxury of making any assumptions about anything. You can never assume that what has worked for you in the past will work for you in the present or future. You cannot assume that any of the change variables are the same. As a community college leader, if you are able to understand, appreciate, plan for, and even anticipate these institutional and board differences— even when you are part of that difference—your odds of success improve.

Additionally, as part of any change initiative, you must convey to the board and other constituents that you fully endorse the change or innovation, and that you will not be dissuaded at the first, second, third, or fourth sign of resistance. Just like the president, the board of trustees has a reputation, which must be preserved.

No board wants to deal with the aftermath of a change initiative gone bad. Let trustees know that you have their backs, that you have done your homework, that you and your team are well prepared, that you are "all in." Either you believe in, and are deeply committed to, what you are proposing, or you don't. If you do, go the distance.

Through experiences like the one discussed above, and the tempering of thirty-five years of research and personal experience in higher education, I have developed a pragmatic, broad, and flexible framework for improving the likelihood of successfully advancing change in organizations (as shown in figure 3.2). Graphically portrayed as a sailboat and based upon my love of the sport, the model depicts a change and innovation Strategy Archetype for Innovation and Leading (SAIL) to provide a conceptual understanding of essential practices for implementation.

Taken together, the elements of the diagram illustrate that in order to sail upon the sea of opportunities toward change and innovation, the captain must have a full and sturdy sail, meaning each of the battens (strategically placed, stackable support systems) must be in place and fully deployed.

From a nautical perspective, "battens" are long strips of sturdy wood or fiberglass that are sleeved within horizontal pockets of the sail to give it strength and rigidity, preventing it from flapping uselessly, thereby gathering all available wind energy essential to propel the boat forward. Like sail battens, the four essential components of leading change and innovation (Leadership Preparation, Institutional Preparation, Assessment and Planning, and Execution and Evaluation) provide the structure and the strength for advancing change.

What the graphic does not portray is what sailboat skippers know all too well. Captains cannot and do not control everything. While we may

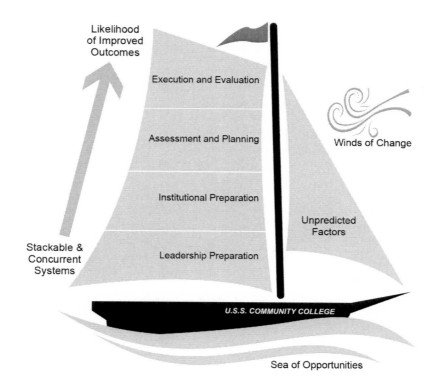

Figure 3.2. Innovation and Change Strategy Archetype for Innovation and Leading (SAIL)

have the latest weather forecasts, best navigational charts, and cutting-edge technology at our disposal, the winds may change direction, gust, slow, or stop completely. We may encounter rough seas or radio communications failure, take on water, get a tear in the mainsail, experience a shortage of provisions, lose the engine, run aground, collide with another vessel, have a fire onboard, lose all electrical systems, grow fatigued, or see a decline in crew morale. We might even doubt our personal resolve and wonder if we should return to our home port.

With so many potential problems, why would anyone want to be a sailboat captain? Well, it's a calling of sorts. Sailors feel called to the sea. In many ways, leading a community college is not dissimilar. It is, for those who are called, a privilege to be in the service of the community and students, to guide them, to teach them, and to help them find the new shores in their lives.

For the remainder of this chapter, and the chapters that follow, I examine the four battens depicted in the SAIL diagram, punctuating and clarifying the purpose of each batten with examples, observations, and experiences. The balance of this chapter focuses specifically on the first-level batten, "Leadership Preparation," which considers board, president, and leadership team readiness and support for a future of change and innovation.

THE VITAL ROLE OF BOARD PREPAREDNESS AND LEADERSHIP IN INNOVATION

Preparing the college for a culture of change and innovation begins at the board level. Through its expressions of policy, mission, and planning documents, and direction to its president, the board declares its intentions. From the very outset, the board, together with the president, must be confident, and in agreement, that the potential benefits of undertaking an institutional strategy of change and innovation are worth the anticipated and unanticipated risks, when compared to the remaining steady-state. To arrive at this conclusion, the board must engage in its own self-assessment and ask essential, introspective questions:

- What kind of future do we envision for our community college?
- How do we intend to respond to the national challenge regarding the completion agenda?
- Are we satisfied with our performance?
- How are we contributing to student failure?
- Why do we still operate with an outmoded, industrial-age business model? What are our options?
- Are we prepared to bear up under any institutional stress that may develop from advancing a culture of innovation?
- How committed are we to this path?
- Do we have the support of key community stakeholders for this new course?
- What are the consequences for our students and our organization if we do not transform our current thinking and related practices?
- What are the consequences for our community if our college does not meet the challenges of a dynamic, highly competitive, global environment?
- Are there thresholds of institutional or board stress that we will not cross?

Essential board leadership requires unembellished honesty in this self-assessment, and a future focus. Trustees must develop a clear frame through which they see their organization, in a process called *generative thinking*.

Authors Richard Chait, William Rayan, and Barbara Taylor describe it as the mental confluence of goal setting and direction setting: "The contributions boards make to mission-setting, strategy-development, and problem-solving certainly shape organizations. But it is cues and frames, along with retrospective thinking, that enable the sense-making on which these other processes depend. A closer examination of nonprofits suggests something else: although generative work is essential to governing, boards do very little of it." [9]

For the first time in the history of our country, the present generation of college-aged U.S. citizens will be less well educated than the generation of their parents. This is a very sad commentary on the effectiveness of our collective work as educators. With so much at stake, regionally and nationally, the board cannot relegate this work nor give only cursory attention to generative thinking about their organization. It is the board who must take responsibility for and lead this work. [10]

However, the board prospers in this work through the early involvement, experience, insight, and utilization of the president and expert consultants, as necessary. The president must assist the board with this work, particularly in the strategy setting for transformative change. The president, in turn, benefits from a clear understanding of the board's position, direction, and expectations. The generative thinking, self-assessment, and goal-setting process is also a great time to clarify the responsibilities of governance and those of the CEO.

A related question that bears asking is what role the board should play in the change process. How involved should they be? An article that appeared in the fall 2014 *MIT Sloan Management Review* asks this essential question. Though focused upon corporate boards, I believe that the research of authors Didier Cossin and Estelle Metayer has direct application to community college boards.

The writers suggest that many boards lack clarity of strategy, which, at best, can result in confusion and, at worst, in operational problems. They recommend a structured assessment of board responsibilities that defines roles early on, with the understanding that these roles might evolve over time.

> In a world where business models are evolving rapidly and new competitors can emerge almost overnight, strategic thinking—especially at the top of the [organization]—is more important than ever to an [organization's] survival. Unfortunately boards have no clear model to follow when it comes to developing the strategic role that is best suited to the [organization] they oversee. At one extreme, the board does little more than rubber-stamp the CEO's decisions, while at the other, the board constantly second-guesses the executive team. Neither adds value." [11]

Optimally, they argue, a board must provide the support and involvement needed, together with the executive, to best meet the organization's needs and strategic priorities. The role of the board must involve three components: 1) Supervisor: monitoring and evaluating executive and organizational performance; 2) Co-creator: contributing to overall strategy by providing insights about the external environment as well as those individual experiences and skills sets; and 3) Supporter: helping the institution avoid pitfalls, garnering support, and assisting the president in his or her work with the government and various constituencies. [12]

Naturally, these roles can be assumed concurrently or independently, change based upon the situation at hand, and evolve over time. The early clarification of the board's role, and that of the president, eliminates any ambiguity regarding responsibilities and intended outcomes. These are crucial inflection points to consider because ultimately it will be the president who transmutes the board's strategic initiatives into action and achievement.

THE PRESIDENT AND PRESIDENTIAL PREPARATION FOR INNOVATION AND CHANGE

Not surprisingly then, the board's first and most important duty is the selection and support of its principal agent of change, the president. It is this single decision that sets the scene for either institutional vibrancy and growth or stagnancy and perhaps decline.

To that end, and as part of its self-assessment, the board must also consider the following questions: Do we agree that the current position description truly represents what we need in our president? Do our goals and expectations for the president accurately convey our intentions for student performance and institutional practices? If we secure a "change master" president, are we prepared to support him or her in the successful adjustment to the culture of this organization? Are we willing to provide the resources necessary for the college president to achieve our ends?

By thoughtfully and favorably considering these questions, the board clarifies for themselves, and for the college president, the tools, means and support by which they will put the college on a good path toward success and competiveness through innovation.

Too often though, the search for and the selection of an institutional leader are unfocused and incongruent with the board's stated future goals, particularly with regard to innovation. The process often follows a predictable, pedantic, and cookie-cutter formula that begins with hiring a consultant to lead the process.

The consultant dutifully engages faculty, staff, administration, alumni, students, the foundation board, and the community in an effort to obtain insights and perspectives regarding the ideal characteristics of the next president. That information is reduced to a "desired leader profile," which is gathered with a variety of institutional and community data, and is subsequently printed on a colorful brochure with scenic campus images, and pictures of a diverse selection of students.

Job advertisements and media announcements trumpet the call for someone who can strategically position the college for the future, establish a culture of innovation, lead change, and propel the college to the next level. The net is cast to sea. The top candidates are pulled from the first catch, run through a lackluster interview process, and a selection is made amid community fanfare.

This process is typical, but it is not optimal. Ideally, in light of its self-assessment, vision, and goal setting toward innovation, the board might consider new strategies for recruitment. Though this work is difficult, to be sure, it is the board's work to do, and, as such, it must not be led by a consultant. Of course a consultant can advise the board and conduct preliminary work, and the board's secretary can assist in the process work. However, the critical determination of skill sets essential to achieve board objectives and candidate appraisal must be done by the board.

In my view, the typical search process used today represents a failed strategy in our changed, competitive reality. This may seem petulant, but ask almost any community college president about the selection process and how effective it was. Ask how many withdrew from a selection process because of how it was handled. You are bound to get an earful. As is widely reported by the American Association of Community Colleges (AACC), the Association of Community College Trustees (ACCT), the American Council on Education (ACE), and other higher education organizations, to further confound matters, the ranks of sitting presidents are dwindling rapidly.

By some measures, another 40 percent of community college presidents are likely to retire by 2020. Indeed, current CEO data from the AACC note that 69 percent of current presidents are fifty-five years of age or older.[13] What's more, many of the administrators in the traditional pathway toward the presidency (e.g., chief academic officers and instructional deans) are either not interested in the top job, or they are retiring along with their president. With competition for talent increasing, and a smaller pool available from which to draw candidates, a fresh approach is required.

In 2014, the Aspen Institute, with support from the Kresge Foundation, published a toolkit to help boards with the selection of a president. Titled "Hiring Exceptional Community College Presidents: Tools for Hiring Leaders Who Advance Student Access and Success," this publication can also be used to evaluate the skill base of the college's current president, and provide suggestions for his or her professional development. The book includes techniques for the hiring process structure, such as a board assessment of college performance, job announcement language, sample behavioral interview scenarios, simulations and questions, as well as a schema for overall assessment of the candidates' institutional fit.[14]

Boards should also be aware of a source of seasoned and proven leaders that may be overlooked. Sitting presidents who may be interested in another post often hesitate to enter a traditional job search since revealing their interest could destabilize the situation at their current institution, perhaps placing their current employment at risk. Consequently, boards may wish to consider the possibility of intentionally scanning the community college landscape for a president who is both experienced and a cultural match for their college, one who could potentially improve their odds of advancing change and innovation.

A trustee representing the board could have an informal conversation with the sitting president of interest, engaging in early, confidential discussions to assess his or her viability as a candidate. This particular approach is not meant to suggest that only experienced presidents can affect change. There are many capable first-time presidents who have done so in prior roles. However, seasoned leaders who have initiated successful change efforts in the past may be a better option for some boards, particularly those governing change-averse, legacy-entrenched colleges. For a first-time president, adjusting to the CEO role and leading institutional innovation at the same time can be a lot to take on.

EXECUTIVE LEADERSHIP AND SUPPORT

When reflecting on the partnership between board and president, I think of essential and regular communications, authenticity, mutual commitment, and support as indispensable tools to advancing a culture of change within an organization. I recall a particularly meaningful interaction I had some years ago at a retreat with the seven-member board of trustees at Jackson College, during which we discussed the support of the president relative to driving institutional change through the contract negotiations process. I said to them, "If I am going to deal with this issue, I want to know that when things get rough, and they will, that when I am pushed back one step, I will feel fourteen hands on my back."

They all agreed. This idea forged a visual image for me, and I believe also for the board, of what it means to be "all in." We established that this was the type of relationship we wanted to have, and I have been grateful for this commitment ever since, as it has made the life of this president much more manageable and pleasant.

As I noted previously in this chapter, for first-time, new-to-a-college, and long-serving presidents alike, boards would be wise to invest in ongoing professional development, particularly in the area of change management. There are a wide variety of avenues for skill building through university-based leadership development programs, such as the

Community College Leadership Program at Iowa State University, the Adult and Community College Education Program at North Carolina State University, and the National American University's Roueche Graduate Center.

These and similar programs offer a more formalized approach to the professional development of senior administrators, with courses such as Community College Leadership, The Community College Presidency, Community College Site-Based Internships, Contemporary Issues in the Community College, Implementing Change Management, Leading Institutional Transformation, and a host of others. Many universities also provide hybrid courses, special certifications, and specialized programming and consulting.

Other programs, like the Presidents Academy Summer Institute (PASI), which is offered each year by the AACC, connect presidents with peers to assist them facilitate their ongoing development and in frank discussion and shared insights. This annual three-day program pairs longer-serving presidents with new presidents to form a system of mentorship.

The programming addresses nationally emerging trends, legislative issues, common institutional challenges, and tools for enhancing the presidency. PASI utilizes focused readings, content experts, case studies, and role playing, and provides a program follow-up for the presidents once they return back home.

In addition to this support, the AACC offers an Executive Leadership Coaching Program and a High Performance Team Training Program to support ongoing professional development and help the president and his or her leadership team to improve their effectiveness. The latter program lasts four days and involves specific training for facilitating change management and related cultural shifts.

GOVERNANCE AND EXECUTIVE INNOVATION LEADERSHIP: IT TAKES TIME

Considering the long-standing traditions of higher education, boards must consider that implementation of change also requires a change within the organization. This implication must be fully considered, understood, and embraced to its logical conclusion. Peter Senge understood not only the value of understanding change, but also the importance of acting upon it: "Organizations incapable of understanding the dimensions of change in their environment and engaging in effective processes to change themselves are risking their very survival." [15]

Cultural change requires campus-wide commitment, which mandates a leader's long-term institutional commitment, which, in turn, is facilitated by the selection of a president whom the board is willing to support for an extended period. Given that the average community college presidency is about four years, and the length of time required for meaningful cultural change to occur is approximately seven years, mutual commitment to leader survival and achievement is vital in the work of change.

In an address to the Michigan Community College Association's Summer Institute in July 2013, president emeritus, Senior League for Innovation in the Community College fellow and distinguished professor and chair of the Graduate Faculty National American University, Terry O'Banion, spoke principally about the national context of the completion agenda.

As part of his remarks, he mentioned the importance of having a forward-thinking, visible, and persistent leader who must champion that agenda, ensuring outcomes. He noted further that this work can only happen when a president has been with an institution for a sufficient and significant length of time, many years, so as to impact cultural and organizational transformation.[16]

Interested to investigate the implications of presidential tenure further, I reached out to colleague Sandy Shugart, president of Valencia College (VC) in Orlando. I was interested in his perspective not only because of his considerable length of service at Valencia, but also because I have observed him successfully integrate change, creativity, vision, and authentic leadership into this higher education space. I hypothesized that in order to adjust institutional culture toward innovation, the president needs to be at the helm for a significant period of time, suspecting that this was a core component that led to, and was validated by, Valencia's Aspen Prize for Community College Excellence in 2011. Shugart affirmed my hypothesis.

> For more than thirty years, I've had a rule of thumb for the tenure of college presidents that says any less than seven years and you are unlikely to get anything meaningful accomplished; any more than ten and you will be running the risk of becoming the new orthodoxy in the way of constructive change. This doesn't mean there aren't outliers, but the exceptions tend to prove the rule. A review of the careers of presidents whose colleges have earned recognition by the Aspen Institute lends substantial evidence to support the rule. But why should this be true? The answer is straightforward. While there are many organizations in the world that need nothing more than a thoughtful strategy and decent execution at an operational level, the nation's community colleges are in need of transformation, and culture is at the center of this work. Reshaping a culture and its deep organizational architecture is a long endeavor, requiring years of engagement with stakeholders, deep inquiry into the nature of the challenge and the prospects for meeting it, and a new covenant among the stakeholders to stick with this work that may endure for many years. Transformational leadership requires endurance, and as Rilke noted, 'endurance comes from . . . enduring.'[17]

Shugart's assertion was confirmed by Jackson Sasser, president of Santa Fe College, Gainesville, Florida, who was the 2015 recipient of the Aspen Prize for Community College Excellence. Having joined the college thirteen years prior, Sasser notes, "I think it really matters how long a president stays at a school. Presidents who make commitments to colleges for some period of time make a difference as opposed to those who use them as stepping stones in their careers. It's got to be the right fit, but if you look at colleges that prosper, that is a factor."[18] All three of these gentlemen intimated that an optimal strategy for innovation to take root is to establish clarity and consensus about the nature and extent of the relationship between the community college president and the board.

Admittedly, most contracts for community college presidents tend to protect the president with a "golden parachute" should they fall out of favor with the board prior to the end of the contract period. However, the board enjoys no such protection should the president choose to leave his or her post before the contract's conclusion. If meaningful and lasting change is to occur at a college, both the board and the president should agree to a long-term covenant, as Shugart asserts—one that is binding and balanced.

For their part, presidents will need contractual confidence to advance board goals by knowing that when issues arise, grievances are filed, votes of no confidence are levied, and news stories are released, the board will be rock solid in its support of the goals and the person it has charged to lead change.

Presidents, in turn, must support their boards even as the board supports them by agreeing to remain at the institution long enough to effect the meaningful change the board seeks. Given a board's interest in creating a sustainable organization, in part through innovation and creativity, there might be an attendant obligation for the president should she or he leave prematurely. At minimum, there should be agreement that an early departure would not be well tolerated by either party. Clearly, such an agreement would need to articulate exceptions. That said, we must minimally acknowledge that the traditional employment arrangement between presidents and boards leaves ample room for improvement.

THE PRESIDENT AND SELF-ASSESSMENT

Presidents, as well as other institutional leaders, should undertake some soul searching as to their own personal and professional risk tolerance, as well as their own shortcomings. Successful community college leaders who have positive and lasting change in their organizations also maintain a capacity to gauge their own levels of preparedness, passion, discipline, hardiness, and weakness, as well as their ability to handle a negative outcome or criticism, should it occur.

A healthy sense of self, personal capacity, agility, and personal honesty regarding the ability to manage the magnitude of a disruptive change are essential as the demands made of the president in his or her commitment to the effort are significant, and they exact a toll. Should ego or pride influence a leader to move forward without the necessary personal fortitude, professional skill set, or ability to involve and engage others, collateral damage will surely follow. It is essential to take the time at the outset to fully consider the difficulty of handling the press, potential personal attacks, and other people sitting in judgment about the undertaking. The time for this self-assessment is not in the middle of a transformative change process.

In the process of innovation and organizational transformation, the work of the president is never complete. Not only are there the ongoing obligations of running the college and its many facets, but the business of change is likewise varied and demanding. In their book *Strategy Rules*, authors David Yoffie and Michael Cusumano consider the leadership strategies of three of the brightest leaders of our day: Bill Gates, Andy Grove, and Steve Jobs. They note that CEOs "need passion, self-confidence, and focus. They need a solid base of knowledge and competence that they can draw on to shape the business and the organization as well as put together a management team."

Gates, Grove, and Jobs did not possess this high level of self-awareness when they first became CEOs. They acquired it over time, sometimes through painful trial and error. But once they understood what they could do and where they needed to rely on others, they became increasingly effective as company leaders.[19]

The authors also mention how all three leaders routinely set aside time for thinking about, and learning, new things. For Andy Grove, learning was one of his highest priorities. Bill Gates set aside a "Think Week" twice a year to withdraw in seclusion to study new ideas, topics, environmental factors, and the future of Microsoft.

On one particular week, Gates reviewed 112 articles on topics such as the theory of language, customer service, and computer science trends in education.[20] This is not to say that community college presidents need to routinely cloister themselves to guide their institutions, but in the business of innovation, a commitment to their ongoing development, and that of their organization, is mandatory.

THE PARTNERSHIP OF THE BOARD AND PRESIDENT TOWARD TRANSFORMATIVE CHANGE

As an element of the partnership between presidents and boards of trustees, boards should ensure that they themselves have ample opportunity for professional development. To appreciate the many challenges associated with change and innovation, their continuing development as institutional trustees is imperative.

As representatives of the public, the board will also undoubtedly receive a full measure of criticism when any significant innovation is advanced. The minute the public, union, or others perceive the break in ranks that occurs when a trustee or two buckle under the pressure, the entire project is at risk, as is the relationship between the board and the president. The work of the president must always be to support his or her board, particularly during the work of innovation and change.

From practical experience and work with many trustees and boards over the years, I have developed five touchstones for my work and support of the board of trustees at Jackson College. Optimally, the president, board chair and, ultimately, the full board must build trust and work well together for the health and advancement of all concerned. To that end, these touchstones have helped me to build trust with the board, to prepare for change, and to face operational difficulties. I call them the Phelan Phive, and I offer them here for your consideration and use:

1. Wherever two or more trustees are gathered, there you should also be;
2. Never, never, never surprise your board — communicate regularly;
3. Choose your battles wisely, as not all bumps in the road are hills upon which to die;
4. What one trustee knows, all should know; and
5. Consistently demonstrate humility as president and acknowledge and respect the board's leadership and contribution — always.

While these axioms are fairly easy to remember, they take considerable time and effort, and they have saved my bacon on more than one occasion. As we move through the four SAIL battens in preparation for change, I consider it important to incorporate these ideas, as they have served me well.

A BROADER LOOK AT LEADERSHIP IN THE CHANGE PROCESS

Community college leaders cannot discover the uncharted oceans of higher education by themselves, no matter how skilled or experienced they may be. It is no sign of weakness, or honor lost, for leaders to seek additional help and support. The business of higher education is the business of people. It is the identification, recruitment, and deployment of talent to provide superior educational programs and services. Thus, any discussion about advancing change and innovation must consider the acquisition of talented and future-focused leaders as part of the president's leadership team.

As the board's first priority in advancing innovation is the selection, direction, and support of their president, so, too, must the president's first attention be to the selection, guidance, and support of key staff members within the college. Richard Alfred, Christopher Shults, Ozan Jaquette, and Shelley Strickland note that community colleges operating in the present reality have little chance for achieving top performance levels unless leadership attends to the business of organizational talent.

In fact, they suggest that the most successful leaders are personally involved as "talent scouts," active in the search for gifted people to join the leadership team, both from outside of the college and within. The idea is to develop a core leadership team that, in turn, will bring others along within the college.[21]

To best determine the type of cabinet-level talent needed, as president you must first consider the areas of knowledge, skills, and abilities that you do not possess but that are essential to organizational transformation. Surrounding yourself with people who can compensate for your areas of weakness will keep you and your institution from a significant and perhaps incapacitating disadvantage, and improve your ability to achieve board and organizational ends.

As suggested by Alfred, Shults, Jaquette, and Strickland, experienced "change-master" presidents know that "people are the most important resource within the organization. In their worldview, organizations are a reflection of the people who work within them, and performance is dictated by people, not resources. Operational efficiency is also important, and it is best achieved through staff who are committed to their job and efficient in their use of time. Change and innovation are a mixed bag for a college . . . some [employees] embrace and innovate as a way of achieving priorities, others prefer the comfort of routine."[22]

It may take time for some presidents who are new to their institutions to cultivate the existing leadership team they inherited, perhaps reassign some of them to other organizational priorities, or remove them from the team altogether. Presidents who have been with their organization for some time may experience this same tension in a different way. Some of your most trusted and talented first-tier leaders may not wish to make the journey to a new innovative environment, in which case they, or you, may need to consider other options for their future. To be sure, making such organizational adjustments can be personally taxing, but it is essential in advancing a new culture.

Case in point: In 2010 I had the distinct pleasure of visiting Poudre Valley Health System in Fort Collins, Colorado, a 2008 recipient of the Malcom Baldrige National Quality Award for performance excellence. Poudre also received the RMPEx Peak Award in both 2004 and 2008, a regional award roughly equivalent to the Baldrige award. I was there as part of a group of about thirty-five other community colleges leaders participating in a Continuous Quality Improvement Network (CQIN) Summer Institute.

Poudre serves the tristate area of northern Colorado, southern Wyoming, and western Nebraska. The hospital is a Level III trauma center with numerous surgical suites and intensive care units, and it offers a regional orthopedic program, cancer treatment, and rehabilitation services. The focus of our visit at Poudre was to better understand how they were able to use quality, accountability, alignment, and integration to improve the organization and achieve higher performance goals.

For me, the most instructive part of the visit was a private meeting we had with Rulon Stacey, Poudre's president and chief executive. I wondered about the specific actions or processes that President Stacey used to fundamentally change the organization. By introducing new levels of quality to a formerly floundering hospital and expanding its operations, he had landed the most coveted national award for excellence. How had he done it? He was mild mannered and deeply committed to providing health care and high quality service to those most in need. I found a man who was a personal and emotional being, trying to do the right thing in his corner of the world. He was not some autocrat or power-hungry CEO.

I asked him about his leadership team and what role they played in the process. Without hesitation, he told us that it was they who were the most essential part of the process, but putting the team in place was also the most difficult part of the process for him personally. He noted that, despite his best efforts, he needed to let some of the core team go, people for whom he cared deeply. In one case, he considered the employee who was involuntarily separated a personal friend. He spoke of the trying work of leadership and how the job may not be for everyone, noting that it needs to be done in as human and honorable a fashion as possible.

I later learned that Poudre Valley joined with the University of Colorado Hospital in early 2012. The combination of an academic hospital with the Poudre Valley Health System created the opportunity to expand both of their reaches even further, taking patient health care to an even higher level and lowering overall costs.

In 2014, Stacey became the president and CEO of Fairview Health Services, located in Minneapolis, Minnesota, and the second largest health organization in the region. While there, he has worked diligently to grow the hospital and improve quality of care, in part through assembling a core team of committed leaders. Today, Rulon Stacy is the Chair of the Board of Overseers for the Malcomb Baldrige National Performance Excellence Program and is a faculty member in the University of Minnasota's Master of Healthcare Administration (MHA) program, actively guiding others toward innovation and quality.

The Poudre Valley example no doubt illustrates how a president can redirect institutional processes and resources, particularly through the right leadership team, to systematically move toward organizational change. Interestingly, the Malcom Baldrige National Quality Award, as part of its semiannual Excellence Framework notification in early 2015, updated its award criteria to include evaluative scoring for organizational elements involving change and innovation, no doubt a recognition by Baldrige of the vital nature of innovation in organizational excellence.

But how does an organization take its leadership team, once gathered, to new heights and help it to develop an innovative ethos? Harvard Business School professor Teresa Amabile interviewed executives and teams in a variety of organizations and arrived at six conditions that must exist for innovation to flourish in a team:

1. There must be demonstrated confidence in the team itself;
2. There must be trust and open communication among team members;
3. The executive is responsible for ensuring that the team members have sufficient responsibility and authority to work toward the targeted goals;
4. Team members need access to necessary resources;
5. Team members need to have challenging responsibilities and assignments; and
6. The executive is responsible for keeping an eye on member stress levels and work pressure, and ensuring realistic timeline for goal achievement.[23]

Amabile's findings are useful for community college presidents at the leadership team level, as well as at the project level. These steps minimally represent a solid foundation upon which community college leaders can build. They also indirectly describe the kinds of conditions that must exist for change and innovation to take root and thrive in a team-based structure.

The bottom line on this discussion about leadership teams is that it is not possible for a president to advance a sustainable climate that supports innovation by himself or herself. Furthermore, no president can hope to singlehandedly generate all the new ideas, services, processes, or programs. No one is that good. Rather, a president needs a solid, dependable, and professional team to extend operational and organizational reach.

It would be a mistake to conclude from the previous discussion that the leadership team should be comprised of only those people who consistently agree with the president, or simply carry out the will of the executive. Quite the opposite is true. The leadership team must include action-oriented, fully engaged individuals who are fearless in offering alternative views and solutions. By so doing, these individuals strengthen the decision making of the president and the likelihood of successful outcomes.

NOTES

1. Maxwell Wessel and Clayton M. Christensen, "Surviving Disruption." *Harvard Business Review* (December 2012): 56–64.

2. Clayton M. Christensen and Henry J. Eyring, *The Innovative University: Changing the DNA of Higher Education from the Inside Out* (San Francisco, CA: Jossey-Bass, 2011), 20.

3. Jeff DeGraff and Shawn E. Quinn, *Leading Innovation: How to Jump Start Your Organization's Growth Engine* (New York: McGraw-Hill Companies, Inc. 2007), 36–37.

4. Daniel James Rowley, Herman D. Lujan, and Michael G. Dolence, *Strategic Change in Colleges and Universities: Planning to Survive and Prosper* (San Francisco, CA: Jossey Bass, Inc., 1997), 173.

5. Nathan Furr and Jeffrey H. Dyer, "Leading Your Team into the Unknown," *Harvard Business Review* (December 2014): 80–88.

6. Ibid.

7. Michael Tushman, "The Ambidextrous Leader: Leadership Tips for Today to Stay in the Game Tomorrow," *IESEinsight* 23 (2014): 31–38.

8. Ibid.

9. Richard P. Chait, William P. Ryan, and Barbara E. Taylor *Governance as Leadership: Reframing the Work of Nonprofit Boards* (Hoboken, NJ: John Wiley & Sons, Inc., 2005), 89.

10. Ibid.

11. Didier Cossin and Estelle Matyer, "How Strategic Is Your Board?" *MIT Sloan Management Review* 56 (2014): 37–44.

12. Ibid.

13. American Association of Community Colleges, "CEO Characteristics." Accessed May 24, 2015. http://www.aacc.nche.edu/AboutCC/Trends/Pages/ceocharacteristics.aspx.

14. Aspen Institute, "Hiring Exceptional Community College Presidents: Tools for Hiring Leaders Who Advance Student Access and Success" (2014). Accessed December 1, 2014. http://www.aspeninstitute.org/publications/hiring-exceptional-community-college-presidents-tools-hiring-leaders-who-advance.

15. Peter Senge, quoted in Suzanne Drapeau, "A Taxonomy of Organizational Change," *Journal of Applied Research in the Community College*, 2 (2004): 81–93.

16. Terry O'Banion, "The Completion Agenda" (presented at the Annual Michigan Community College Association's Summer Institute, Traverse City, Michigan, July 26, 2013).

17. Sandy Shugart, personal communication to author, December 30, 2014.

18. Emily Rogan, "Q & A with Jackson Sasser," *Community College Daily*. Accessed May 1, 2015. http://ccdaily.com/Pages/Campus-Issues/President-of-Aspen-PrizeWinning-College-Discusses.aspx.

19. David B. Yoffie and Michael A. Cusumano, *Strategy Rules: Five Timeless Lessons from Bill Gates, Andy Grove, and Steve Jobs* (New York: HaperCollins Publishers, 2015), 168.

20. Ibid.

21. Richard Alfred et al., *Community Colleges on the Horizon: Challenge, Choice, or Abundance* (Lanham, MD: Rowman & Littlefield Publishers, Inc., 2009), 110.

22. Alfred et al., *Community Colleges on the Horizon: Challenge, Choice, or Abundance*, 181.

23. Jim Biolos, "Six Steps Toward Making a Team Innovative" in *Harvard Management Update* (Boston, MA: Harvard Business School Publishing, 1996).

FOUR

Institutional Preparation and Culture

"It is change, continuing change, inevitable change that is the dominant factor in society today. No sensible decision can be made any longer without taking into account not only the world as it is, but the world as it will be."
—Isaac Asimov

Culture has the power to outmaneuver any organizational change that may be attempted. Culture will overrun anyone who faces it with ignorance, disregard, or antagonism. Change efforts are for naught in the absence of a full reconnaissance of institutional culture and subcultures. This is not to say that strategy is not important, even indispensable. It just cannot exist apart from the cultural and subcultural realities of an organization.

As college leaders prepare their institutions for disruptive, sustaining, or continuous innovation, they need to understand the nuances and multiple dimensions of the current culture and consider methods by which it can be modified to not only support innovation, but endure a steady diet of it.

Organizational culture is a curious concoction of human psychology, beliefs, and behaviors. Therefore, each culture has its own thumbprint. Kim Cameron and Robert Quinn characterize culture this way:

> [Culture is] . . . the taken-for-granted values, underlying assumptions, expectations, collective memories, and definitions present in an organization. It represents "how things are done around here." It reflects the prevailing ideology that people carry inside their heads. It conveys a sense of identity to employees, provides unwritten and often unspoken guidelines for how to get along in the organization, and it helps stabilize the social system that they experience. Unfortunately, people are unaware of their culture until it is challenged, until they experience a new culture, or until it is made overt and explicit. . . . At the most

fundamental level, culture is manifest as the implicit assumptions that define the human condition and its relationship to the environment.[1]

Wherever there is more than one employee, an organizational culture becomes coded in the institutional DNA. It is important to emphasize that in most organizations there is not just one culture, but many subcultures as well, each with their own dialect of values, beliefs, and mores. Employee reactions to a new idea—for example, the adaptation of a four-day workweek—may vary significantly from building to building or from campus to campus, by job classification or department, or by employee demographic groups. To lump all employees into a single, homogeneous culture is misguided and problematic.

Higher education cultures will often actively dissuade the contemplation, let alone the implementation, of new ideas in favor of time-honored practices. The obvious danger associated with this paradigm paralysis is that institutions become complacent with the way things are, content in being "good enough." The combination of cultural norms, including shared governance, academic freedom, and labor agreements, creates a difficult space for innovation to take root.

Author and former Stanford University Graduate School of Business Professor Jim Collins asserts that employees' perceptions of their organization as being "good" are, in fact, the enemy of potential greatness in any organization.[2] In some cases, historical accomplishments contribute to a "numbing effect," which impedes long-term excellence. An award here, a national recognition there, and accolades in local media are validations that lead some institutions to become satisfied, and, in turn, they may build dams instead of doing everything possible to increase the flow of innovation through the organization.[3]

In the highly competitive environment of higher education, a college's past success guarantees nothing for the future. The constant quest for excellence, innovation, and marketplace relevance is simply the price of admission. A community college's value is, and should be, measured by its quality, service to the consumer, and achievements only for today. Tomorrow is always up for grabs.

Business author Steve Denning observed that when change is attempted in an organization, a powerful force presses it toward its prior state the way a strong storm drives water further inland, only to have it settle back into its basin. Change sparks a lot of activity, movement, and noise. However, if culture isn't intentionally designed, it will be difficult to sustainably influence. Denning offers the staying power of culture as one of the chief reasons that leaders don't undertake change. He notes:

> An organization's culture comprises an interlocking set of goals, roles, processes, values, communication practices, attitudes, and assumptions. The elements fit together as a mutually reinforcing system and combine to prevent any attempt to change it. That's why single-fix

changes, such as the introduction of teams, or Lean, or Agile, or Scrum, or knowledge management, or some new process, may appear to make progress for a while, but eventually the interlocking elements of the organizational culture take over and the change is inexorably drawn back into the existing organizational culture.[4]

Still, some community colleges have cracked the code of this cultural interlock and maintained momentum in their innovation. One such organization is Rio Salado College in Tempe, Arizona, part of the Maricopa Community College System. From its beginnings in 1978, this "college without walls" was created to provide educational programming to nontraditional students at a distance. By 1995, the college had embraced the Internet as a modality to scale distance learning.

Today Rio Salado provides innovative, low-cost, online courses in the greater Phoenix metropolitan area. Under the leadership of President Chris Bustamante, the college continues to act as a prototype for innovation. For example, the RioAchieve program, funded by the Bill and Melinda Gates Foundation, is designed to target five specific interventions that support student success, retention, and completion.

These interventions are delivered through technological innovations that allow them to be scaled. Given the potential applications of this innovation for higher education, the former Microsoft president and co-chair of the foundation, Bill Gates, Jr., visited the campus in 2014 to better understand the program and the drivers of its success.[5]

What is it about the culture at Rio Salado that sustains this focus on innovation? President Bustamante explained to me that part of its approach is to rethink the collaborative nature of employee relationships and support people working in teams and across silos. He also indicated that the college has improved its relationships with other universities, vendors, and external organizations.

Bustamante believes that the future will bring colleges and companies even closer as they collectively evolve with a focus on student success. For example, he cited a fee-based pilot partnership with Civitas Learning in which Rio and other participating colleges share student demographics and performance data with Civitas Learning for their use. The company then returns analytics that administrators can use to align support services for their student populations. Bustamante noted that as he introduces new initiatives, he is constantly mindful of the college's culture:

> If our teams are going to be open to innovation, you have to acknowledge that the traditional methods won't work and help [employees] understand that in a supportive way. I believe the source of many of the innovative ideas will continue to come from the voice of the customer, so we have to listen. Competency-based education, modularization, credit for prior learning, and other similar advances, are solutions driven by customer need.[6]

Bustamante argued further that "New Frontier Community Colleges' will be defined by paying attention to the internal and cultural environment, engaging employees, monitoring the horizon, and blazing trails while others are just trying to catch up."[7] Rio Salado is a college that understands the SAIL second batten—Institutional Preparation. It gets the importance of assessing the marketplace and environment, including its internal culture. This college will continue to be one to watch in the years ahead.

The partnership between Rio and Civitas Learning is one manifestation of the emergent, deliberate trend of community colleges working collectively and in partnership with private, for-profit organizations to the benefit of the whole. One such organization is the Higher Education Research and Development Institute (HERDI).

HERDI President Toni Cleveland, herself a former community college president at Niagara County Community College, brings together some of the nation's best community college presidents with company representatives for intensive and deliberative discussions about the development of products and services to better serve the needs of higher education.

The results of these panels have provided mutual benefits. In some cases, companies have modified their products to provide a better pathway to the market. In other cases, they have avoided unnecessary spending on a product or service that would likely be unsuccessful. Presidents, in turn, get an early, inside look at the way the industry is moving, which can help them to better position their organizations for the future.

In some cases, pilot programs have been established to test a new product or service at a community college campus, which has not only refined the company's plans, but also provided the college an opportunity to evaluate the product or service within its organization.

While confidentiality precludes me from providing specific examples of products and services discussed in the panels and the associated outcomes, I can tell you that HERDI reflects the change to consultative, collaborative relationships that foster mutual success between colleges and strategic partners. Forging a critical dialogue about the future of community colleges, markets, products, and services makes infinite sense at a time when most of the nation's community colleges have limited resources available to find or fund the future on their own.

ORGANIZATIONAL CULTURE, SOCIALIZATION, AND LEARNING

Too often, community college leaders do not spend the time necessary to fully understand the socialization process within the organization, and the ways in which employees assign meaning to their environment. I have found that the selection of new employees, an effective onboarding process, and ongoing cultural cultivation are the three most important actions that any institution undertakes.

Michael Kramer describes the importance of understanding the sense-making experience for new employees in an effort to better understand how individuals experience their environment. Within this socialization process, Kramer notes that interorganizational communication is the principal driver of meaning formation.[8]

While it can be stunning how quickly new personnel are co-opted by the current cultural regime, it can also represent a fresh opportunity to redirect the organization to a preferred cultural course. It is possible to frame the vision, define the relationship, build connections, and obtain commitment from new hires, but it requires focused and persistent effort. It is essential, therefore, that the president be specific about the goals, content, and outcomes of the first few days, weeks, and months of an employee's tenure. This initial period should be designed for the type of institution you aspire to become. The process and substance of orientation, the initial formation of relationships, and the guidance provided will determine the fate of your institution and your future as its leader.

To begin, community college leaders must recognize that an employee's socialization begins well before he or she is hired. This is called "anticipatory socialization." Optimally, though not always, this is what draws potential employees to a college. An institution's reputation and culture are widespread, whether intentionally or unintentionally, through newspaper articles, social media, and community dialogue. It is therefore vital that the human resources and marketing offices periodically review these materials with a focused lens on cultural messaging for new employees. Even official letters and materials will serve as critical socialization clues.

Take a moment and ask the people who cross your path in the course of your day, perhaps even some of your own employees, about their experience of being hired. More often than not, they will reveal that they were hired with little attention to their onboarding or need for ongoing support, and that they felt less connected over time as a result. The onboarding process experienced by many employees is haphazard.

In numerous cases, the employee's first day on the job feels unsettled and unsettling. Their offices are not ready, phones are not installed, computers are not connected, and, in some cases, the supervisor isn't even at the office. Often the procedure involves little more than paperwork, a brief introduction to some coworkers, and a tour of the workstation. Then the employee is left to figure things out on his or her own.

Kramer notes that the newcomer's first days are difficult, stressful, and uncertain, and this impacts him or her for the long term. "Research to date suggests that what organizations and individuals do in the organizational socialization process can make a big difference with respect to a variety of important outcomes including employee satisfaction, commitment, retention, and performance."[9] This process can make the difference between the employee quickly adapting to the dominant culture and behaving accordingly, or embracing a new approach to innovation and serving as an active player in the change agenda.

This attention to the onboarding process must begin as early as when job announcements and job descriptions are created. The interview should be behaviorally focused, evidence based, and absent the more traditional elements, such as allowing the candidate to speak in generalities. Assessing skill through observation, simulation, discussion, or presentation is all worthwhile. However, the college should assess more than applicants' skill sets.

It is important to include atypical assessments, such as motivational fit queries and structured behavioral questioning, and to dig deeper in general. Crowdsourced references, current employer visits, communications sampling, and a work portfolio review are some ways to discern cultural and organizational fit. The secret to organizational redesign is to get the right people on the bus: committed people who can adapt to a fast-paced, constantly changing industry, and then to get these team members in the right seats on the bus.[10] In my view, most mistakes in the hiring process are made due to a poorly constructed interviewing and assessment process. It must not be forgotten that one single hire can be a million-dollar decision, or more.

Consider the work of Zappos, the online shop for name-brand shoes and clothing. Each year, the company has literally tens of thousands of applications for a few hundred jobs. This is not surprising since Zappos has an exciting, innovative, can-do culture.[11] To be considered for employment, candidates must pass an initial telephone screening process wherein a determination is made as to whether the candidate's personality aligns with the culture of the company.

If successful, the candidate speaks with another human resources professional whose job is to assess the candidate's specific skill sets and his or her ability to do the job. Candidates then take two tests to evaluate their overall capabilities. If their scores meet the requirements, applicants are asked to visit the company for a day-long meeting, which includes multiple interviews, appraisals, lunch with staffers, tours, and other activities, all designed to provide a robust assessment of the candidate and his or her potential fit.

If selected, candidates are advanced to a four-week training program. Zappos considers this training to be part of the employee assessment process, and if at any point a candidate seems unengaged or out of alignment with company culture, he or she is given $2,000 and excused. The organization is very serious about the value and contribution of each employee, so it invests in recruitment, cultural congruence, and retention—and it works. Voluntary turnover is about 8 percent.[12]

The bottom line regarding orientation is that the president needs to translate the wishes of the board, set the tone for the college's direction, establish expectations for employee behavior, and obtain a commitment to the institution's goals. Characteristically, community colleges with a solid culture of innovation also have a strategic, purposeful, and meaningful onboarding process. Not every process will match the extensive and expensive approach of Zappos'; however, key touchstones will likely include the following:

1. Make new employees feel like part of the family before they show up. Send a card to their home from you and the leadership team, or send a "goodie bag" or college t-shirt. Don't make the mistake of thinking electronic communication is enough. Make it as personal as possible.

2. Send out an e-mail to everyone in the office or college, as appropriate, so they're prepared to welcome new employees.

3. Greet and welcome every new employee upon arrival at the college. Make the first day memorable. Focus on the experience and emotional takeaway.

4. Introduce new employees to key people within the college and provide an opportunity for them to get to know each other.

5. Help new employees learn names and roles. Share an organizational chart of their department that spells out who's responsible for what (with photos). Include people the new employee will likely encounter, and to whom they might turn for help, for example, with IT issues.

6. Introduce new employees to the person who will be their mentor for the next twelve months. The mentor should serve as their key contact, beyond their supervisor.

7. Carefully guide new employees through the human resources paperwork process, employee manuals, and orientation documents.

8. Give new employees a tour of campus and campus facilities.

9. Invite new employees to college events and introduce them to people there.

10. Take them to lunch on the first day or two.

11. Set up their office and leave a welcoming gift. Provide a name plate on their desk or office door as a tangible sign that you've prepared the space.

12. Have a stack of business cards waiting.

13. Make sure new employees understand the employee evaluation process, and their goals and objectives for the next six- and twelve-month periods.

14. If they are not from the community, invite them to a few community events, and introduce them to people there.

This entire process should be orchestrated over the first few days and weeks of the new employee's tenure. Additionally, the college should employ "orientation booster shots" or ongoing cultural cultivation over subsequent months and years to ensure that new recruits are provided a balanced environment in which they can form their own opinions. To make sure we live up to the promises we have made to new employees, it is also important to check in regularly with employees to ensure that our goals for onboarding and staff development are consistent with the employee experience.[13]

I have to confess that I haven't always gotten this right as a college leader. Most of us, particularly those of us at smaller institutions, are hyperstretched for time, pulled toward the most pressing need of the moment. Regrettably, from time to time, a few such issues have flared higher and taken precedence over attending to these critical first moments of cultural adaptation, and I didn't take responsibility for it.

Instead, I grew frustrated by the fact that new employees did not grab the ropes on our boat, trim the sails, and "heave-ho" as I had hoped, regardless of the promise and commitment we thought they had made around the interview table. Many of them fell victim to the dominant culture, which maintained that change was a bad thing. I realized that I had to do more than share a vision and provide encouragement. We needed structure, focus, clarity, support, and accountability. I resolved to change.

Specifically, the Leadership Council (the president's cabinet) and I prioritized talent acquisition and engaged in a number of professional development activities, incorporating planning sessions, retreats, survey data, benchmarking, assigned readings, visioning, and heart-felt discussions about the college's direction, and our roles within it. I asked the council to join me at a Continuous Quality Improvement Network (CQIN) in Boston in 2013. That year, the theme was "Using Systems Thinking as a Catalyst to Drive Breakthrough Change."

We heard speeches by Peter Senge, director of the Center for Organizational Learning at the MIT Sloan School of Management, as well as from representatives of Bridgeway Partners, Northwestern Mutual Insurance, and the Creative Learning Exchange. We learned about tools and practices essential for incorporating systems thinking as a catalyst for change, and we identified key barriers at Jackson College.

Over the following twelve months we implemented a number of systems, including a reboot of our hiring methodology. We attended the CQIN conference again in 2014 in St. Louis. This time the theme was "Creating High Engagement among Faculty and Staff to Optimize Work Systems and Improve Organizational Performance." There we heard from a number of learning partners, including the Ritz Carlton, Nestle Purina Pet Care Company, and Headwinds, Ltd. These conferences, and the dedicated planning time with the Leadership Council, were extraordinary for me in that we not only gelled as a team, but that we also committed our best selves to the work that needed to be done.

We drew up plans based upon best practices, our research, and our professional development. We put together a design to appropriately staff the human resources office to handle the increased workload attendant to a world-class selection, hiring, onboarding, and nurturing process. The Leadership Council concluded that as keepers of the culture, and the responsible party for achievement of strategic goals, we would be the final authority in the selection of new employees. To that end, we asked all institutional hiring committees to forward their recommendations to the Leadership Council for consideration.

Today the council reviews the resumes, job descriptions, and committee selection notes for all full- and part-time permanent postings, and we also interview each final candidate. At that stage, we assume that the candidate's technical skills have been duly vetted by the prior selection committee and the candidate's would-be supervisor. The meeting with the Leadership Council is more of a dialogue through which we evaluate whether candidates exemplify our values, beliefs, and quest for innovation and creativity.

We ask them about their personal journey. We ask them to explain how their beliefs, values, and behaviors align with our institution, using specific examples. In some cases, the council has declined the recommendation to hire a candidate and charged the hiring committee to recast the net. This process takes considerable time from the college's leaders, but we ask ourselves what could be more important to our objective of sustaining an innovative institution?

On those occasions when a candidate is selected to join us, he or she is required to undergo five full days of onboarding before ever beginning the job, without exception. This onboarding activity is held the second week of each month, with all new part-time and full-time employees fully participating.

The new employee's first week begins with a review of the mission, values, and beliefs of the college and lunch with the president, followed by tours of each campus and a technology orientation. During lunch with the new employees, I invite them to send me e-mails during their first few months with the label "newbie idea." The point is to get their fresh observations before they become fully acculturated. I use those e-mails to help refine our practices.

The balance of the introductory week includes meetings with the Leadership Council, a review of job duties and expectations, instructional and facility plans, an orientation on safety and security, a review of program budgets and goals, meetings with all college departments, lunch with the college's board chair, and a host of other items. Each NEO (new employee onboarder) is required to attend one board of trustees meeting within the first two months. Additionally, each NEO is assigned a mentor who will provide continuing support and guidance during the first year of employment.

For the next four years, each new faculty member will meet annually with the Leadership Council prior to being awarded a continuing contract. Similarly, all support staff will meet with the Leadership Council after five months and prior to their being awarded permanent employment. Members of college administration also meet with the council near the end of their first- and second-year anniversaries.

During these meetings, the Leadership Council addresses the satisfaction of the employees, their relationship with their supervisors, and the impact they are having on the institution. It's also a time to explore the employee's demonstration of commitment to the college's beliefs. If the council concludes that there is a strong congruence with the preferred culture of the college, the employee is retained. If not, the employee is released from further obligation.

The principal goal of each of these steps is to lay a new foundation upon which we establish innovation and relevance in the service of students. Retirements, departure of employees who are uncomfortable with the institutional direction, and the onboarding of new, culturally malleable employees all facilitate the desired culture shift.

ASSESSING THE CURRENT CULTURAL ENVIRONMENT

Although not all of an organization's cultural characteristics are immediately apparent, there are a number of methods that can be used to make an evaluation. One of the quicker tools is a cultural audit, sometimes referred to as a "climate survey." This type of assessment is performed through the solicitation of anonymous information, perspectives and perceptions of employees, and customers regarding organizational values, behaviors, and practices, all in an effort to determine if college actions support or undercut its mission and expressed goals.

A number of formal instruments are available to accomplish this. Cameron and Quinn cite the Organizational Culture Assessment Instrument (OCSI) as the most utilized and accurate tool for evaluating culture, having been used in a variety of industry sectors. It is based upon the Competing Values Framework and considers six dimensions of organizational culture: Dominant Characteristics, Organizational Leadership, Management of Employees, Organizational Glue, Strategic Emphasis, and Criteria for Success. [14]

Based upon their research of over thirty years, authors Jay Rao and Joseph Weintraub also compiled a list of six dimensions of innovation, though theirs function as building blocks and include the following:

- Resources—people, systems, and projects;
- Processes—the methods by which innovation is advanced;

- Values—what drives decision making and priorities;
- Behavior—how people act in the pursuit of innovation;
- Climate—the overall energy and feel of the workplace; and
- Success—comprised of three categories: personal, enterprise, and external validation.

The authors developed the Innovation Quotient, a cultural survey built upon an expansion of these six blocks into fifty-four elements, the results of which provide a sense of areas of change resistance within an organization. [15]

Another model is the Personal Assessment of the College Environment (PACE), which is administered by North Carolina State University's (2014) National Initiative for Leadership and Institutional Effectiveness (NILIE) Center. The survey focuses on obtaining the perceptions of employees, and the data assist colleges in advancing open communication among employee groups.

The Hay Group (2014) is yet another organization that assesses the health of organizational climate. The company has been utilizing its Organizational Climate Survey (OCS) for over forty years to help leaders evaluate an organization's readiness for change, as well as employee effectiveness, motivational practices, employee responsibility levels, leader empathy, and communication.

These and other instruments provide modest customization by reserving some portion of the survey for specific questions of interest to the college. Another more personalized option is for a college to develop its own "home-grown" assessment, which can be administered through the human resources office or institutional research department. Colleges can use simple and customizable online systems like SurveyMonkey to quickly, easily, and cheaply gather important institutional information. In using a home-grown system, it is important to dedicate sufficient time to developing relevant and evocative questions. To lend further value to the institution, the instrument should be used at regular intervals in order to demonstrate trends.

Waubonsee Community College (WCC) in Illinois has recognized the importance of assessing culture and has capitalized on its newfound understanding. President Christine Sobek and her leadership teams sought to better attract, develop, and retain employees who were committed to the goals of the college, especially as talented employees began to retire. A concomitant goal was to build a culture focused upon success. [16]

Sobek noted that success looks different for each employee, and employees tend to pursue their own vision. As part of the process, the leaders assessed the WCC culture and level of employee engagement. Sobek remarked, "We wanted to make employee engagement a daily priority, and build a culture of trust." [17]

WCC created a steering committee that encompassed many areas of the college. They partnered with a neighboring community college interested in the same goal, and subsequently engaged a consultant and implemented a survey. The resulting data were openly shared with employees, and post-hoc focus groups were used to further evaluate survey findings.

Incorporating this work as part of its ongoing accreditation process, the college's Academic Quality Improvement Project (AQIP) action teams created three Employee Engagement Teams to validate survey results, identify major themes, and recommend areas of focus. One outcome designed to connect employees, for example, was that all personnel were strongly encouraged to wear college-provided nametags in an effort to build familiarity among staff, and connections with students, across all buildings and campuses. The college's leadership group modeled the behavior, rather than simply mandating the action.

Additionally, WCC has enhanced its communications efforts, encouraged employee engagement through service on committees and projects, and intentionally practiced broad-based collaboration toward institutional goals. The college regularly monitors its culture and development with follow-up surveys, which are administered every three years. The overarching initiative of cultural improvement is appropriately titled "Embracing Engagement: Connect, Collaborate, and Cultivate."

Continuous assessment is important because modifying culture is largely contingent upon having a sense of employees' perceptions of how the college cares about them as individuals, whether the president really knows what it is like to be in their jobs, whether and to what extent their opinion and work really matters, and whether there is joy in the workplace. The attention of leadership to its most valuable asset—its people—through understanding, appreciation, and careful transitions is not only respectful, but also an advantageous strategy. We must not underestimate the impact of engaging employees in the change process, recognizing and valuing their contributions, offering support, and empathizing with them.

Employees are generally mindful that they spend more time at the workplace than they do with their loved ones. If the environment is subpar by their estimation, they will come to work each day in a difficult space, alongside other unhappy people, and negativity will quickly become pervasive. Of course, there will be organizational stresses in unique and isolated instances, such as contract negotiations, loss of an institutional leader, or enrollment decline, but a typical day at the college speaks as much to the organizational culture as do these instances of tension.

Organizations such as the Chronicle of Higher Education have begun to grant distinctions to celebrate institutional culture, such as their compilation of "Great Colleges to Work For." In this particular example, survey URL links are sent to randomly selected employees, including adjunct faculty, of those colleges and universities that agree to participate. The survey probes for information, including employees' overall satisfaction in areas such as diversity, supervisors, culture, and environment. Community colleges are categorized as large, medium, and small, based on their enrollment, and organizations are recognized within each group. [18]

On one level, this type of survey provides institutional incentive to improve overall climate, especially as this distinction may increase an institution's appeal to potential employees in an increasingly competitive market. Yet on another level, colleges facing institutional stress may be unlikely to participate, thereby rendering the process self-selecting. This type of program is a good indicator of employee satisfaction, but by itself, it is insufficient. A college can have satisfied employees because of benefits, workload, or work environment, but still they may be unengaged in the heavy lifting necessary for adaptation to an innovative culture.

THE POWER OF CULTURE TO DISRUPT INNOVATION AND CHANGE

Roger Connors and Tom Smith, well-known authors and cofounders of Partners in Leadership, Inc., note that culture holds the key to your ability to advance organizational change. Left to its own devises, culture will impede your every effort. As the organizational leader, you have two choices. Abdicate your responsibilities and allow culture to disrupt your efforts and to manage you and your college, or define a preferred cultural environment and work intently to achieve and nurture it. The authors state:

> In our work, we continually meet people, at every level of an organization, who get batted around by their company's culture. Their culture undermines their attempts to get the results they want. They long for stronger customer focus, but they can't get it. They appreciate the need for regulatory compliance, but they can't attain it. They plan for growth, quality, productivity and profitability, only to end up disappointed by a lack of performance. When the culture is not working, it poses a formidable obstacle to achieving results. [19]

Rowley and Sherman concur, noting that from the perspective of the academy, people feel that they "have the right to behave as they believe to be best. Various campus constituents believe that they have built their college or university over time and that the institution stands as a testament to the 'rightness' of their efforts and of those who have gone before. . . . If campus leaders and planners do nothing to address this concern, the full weight of the powerful culture can become a formidable block to change." [20]

On one particular occasion, I recall feeling the presence of the intransigent nature of culture like the strike of a sailboat's boom swinging quickly across the boat in a change of course. It occurred a few years after changing economic conditions caused a national decline in community college enrollment. Jackson College was no exception, and we were unfortunately forced to reduce employment levels.

Culture appeared palpably during a meeting to outline staffing reduction plans. One of our unionized staff members articulated a widely held cultural belief, one that I had somehow overlooked. "We were supposed to have this job for life! Jackson College never lays people off or fires anyone. Ever!" You can imagine, I'm sure, the amount of institutional and public consternation that followed. There it was, the power of culture disrupting the direction forward. But how did I not see it earlier?

As it turns out, she was right. Historically, the college had rarely laid anyone off for any reason, including poor work performance. This deeply held belief was buttressed by two union groups actively working to leverage the cultural norm, giving their members a stronger sense of protection. The union contract included a number of interesting provisions.

For one, it required the elimination of anything negative or poor-performance-related in the employee's personnel file after two years. Consequently, over time, there was no motivation to pull hard on the lines, address the changing needs of our industry, or make any changes. I later learned that due to the commonly held belief that the college never let anyone go, some administrators were submitting performance evaluations of their staff in a substandard manner. Under this premise, administrators understandably concluded that it was a waste of time to conduct extensive evaluations, or even to detail employee performance in annual reports. Many completed the evaluation by simply checking the "meets expectations" box, and offered no additional narrative.

As a result, when needed in the course of due diligence, performance reviews turned up nothing but glowing or average performance evaluations, regardless of employees' past performance. In some cases, evaluations had not even been completed at all. Interestingly, when speaking in a private meeting, supervisors would readily reveal the actual, though unrecorded, employee history to human resource officials. This information was, of course, useless in the absence of proper documentation, which was extremely frustrating for anyone committed to data-driven decision making. A deep-seated cultural belief had created a behavioral blockade through which nothing could pass.

Armed with new cultural understanding, the college's Leadership Council and I aimed to modify our culture in an enduring way. Like most of their kind, our mission, vision, and values statements were high-minded, broad, and noble sounding, designed to adorn boardrooms and satisfy accreditors. We decided to go deeper. We decided to pronounce what we would stand for and what we would not. We gathered ideas from students, employees, community members, peers, alumni, and foundation members. We drafted common thoughts, and distributed them broadly and repeatedly until we found a general consensus on language. The result was a statement of beliefs,[21] approved by the board of trustees, and it appears in figure 4.1.

As Employees of Jackson College, We Believe:
• The success of our students is always our first priority;
• We must perform our jobs admirably, giving our best service and support every day, for everyone;
• Teamwork is founded upon people bringing different gifts and perspectives;
• We provide educational opportunities for those who might otherwise not have them;
• In providing employees with a safe and fulfilling work environment, as well as an opportunity to grow and learn;
• Our progress must be validated by setting goals and measuring our achievements;
• We must make decisions that are best for the institution as a whole;
• Building and maintaining trusting relationships with each other is essential;
• Competence and innovation are essential means of sustaining our values in a competitive marketplace;
• We make a positive difference in the lives of our students, our employees, and our communities;
• In the principles of integrity, opportunity and fairness;
• We must prepare our students to be successful in a global environment; and
• Our work matters.

Figure 4.1.   Jackson College Statement of Beliefs

All final candidates for employment at Jackson College are presented with these beliefs, and the beliefs are reviewed and discussed as part of the interview process. Ultimately, candidates are asked if they would agree to be held accountable to these beliefs—in order to be employed, a candidate must sign off on his or her commitment to them. We emphasize that the beliefs must be taken together, not treated as a smorgasbord, in which it is possible to commit to some but not others.

This list is reviewed at the beginning of staff meetings and convocations, and it pops up on employees' computer screens when they turn them on in the morning. The beliefs also comprise a part of annual performance reviews for all employees—union member or not—as outlined in the new union contract. And in order to improve effectiveness in conducting employee evaluations, we implemented monthly professional development for all supervisors at the college.

It has been a slow, protracted process, but the college has begun to see lasting employee commitments, increasing peer accountability, and a recognition that continued employment is contingent on demonstrating the college's beliefs daily. While to do so won't guarantee lifelong employment, it does increase the likelihood of retention by creating a common understanding and expectation for high-quality service for all in the organization.

In fact, I have noticed a particular appreciation for this work from our hardest-working employees, as they now see that everyone is held to the same standard. As John Kotter, former professor of Harvard's Business School and renowned expert on business leadership, noted, "Culture changes only after you have successfully altered people's actions, after the new behavior produces some group benefit for a period of time, and after people see the connection between the new actions and the performance improvements."[22]

To achieve this end, suggest Connors and Smith, a leader must instill accountability within, and for the culture he or she seeks to create. They describe a demarcation between accountable and nonaccountable behavior: accountability is framed by the actions of "See It, Own It, Solve It, and Do It"[23] and is considered an "above the line" behavior. Unacceptable, or "below the line" behavior is fraught with blaming others and accepting no personal responsibility.

They explain, "Above the Line Accountability lays the foundation for a Culture of Accountability, in which people take accountability to think and act in the manner necessary to achieve organizational results. No other culture works as well to ensure success."[24] Since the culture of an organization is either going to work for or against the president, developing culture and seeking evidence of this development is the only option for presidents to be successful.

After extensive research with a number of national and international companies, Kotter developed five key anchors of lasting cultural change: 1) The bulk of cultural change presents itself at the end of the transformation process, not in the early stages; 2) New approaches only survive after their relative success has been benchmarked against the old processes and found to be superior; 3) Regular, consistent communication of the initiative and outcomes is essential; 4) If evaluation and promotion actions are not reflective nor supportive of the new methodology, the old practices will reemerge; and 5) Despite best efforts and working with employees through the transition, occasionally some employees will not make the journey, and their skill sets will be freed up for use by the competition.[25] If these steps are not duly regarded during a change process, the leader will unnecessarily disrupt the organization, expend resources, and likely lose ground in the present and any future change process.

Community colleges are in a better strategic position for improvement when they engage in continuous quality improvement (CQI) evidence-based practices, utilizing key performance indicators (KPIs), balanced scorecards, and routine documentation of institutional productivity. For community colleges unfamiliar or uncomfortable with making lasting cultural shifts, a number of organizations are available to help with the journey. The Continuous Quality Improvement Network (CQIN), as mentioned previously for their work combining community college leaders with business standouts for collaboration and study, is one such example.

RECOGNIZING THE URGENCY FOR CULTURAL ADAPTATION TO INNOVATION

Cultural adaptation to any major change takes courage, conviction, and discipline based upon a sense of urgency in order to remain relevant. It must be advanced by design, not circumstance or happenstance, and at a pace designed to ensure the long-term success of the organization. The literature across industries is replete with examples in which leaders and organizations could not see a game-changing force or circumstance coming, or failed to move with dispatch to adapt the dominate culture to one engaging an environment replete with new and emerging competitors.

In one industry, for example, Saul Kaplan notes that the once ubiquitous, entrepreneurial Blockbuster Video entered into the annals of corporate and customer irrelevance because the company's culture was not prepared to adapt to constant changes in technology. Former CEO John Antioco could not conceptualize the value proposition of doing so. Netflix seized the opportunity borne of Blockbuster's complacency and leveraged DVDs, the postal system, and the Internet to create a disruptively innovative business model in the delivery of entertainment to homes, iPads, and computers everywhere, for just a few dollars per movie.

As Kaplan describes it, Blockbuster got "Netflixed."[26] Netflix has continued to adapt and anticipate the market. In fact, the company has since extended its reach to the development of their own content. In early 2013 the company created a television political drama series, *House of Cards*, and it has others on the drawing board. The company has launched in Cuba in 2015 and looks to penetrate the markets in China and Japan in the near future.

This Netflix example confirms Clayton Christensen's message regarding companies whose culture and action limit ongoing improvement to their current product or service. He notes that companies stay with "what has historically helped them succeed: by charging the highest prices to their most demanding and sophisticated customers at the top of the market, companies will achieve the greatest profitability. However, by doing so, companies unwittingly open the door to 'disruptive innovations' at the bottom of the market. An innovation that is disruptive allows a whole new population of consumers at the bottom of a market access to a product or service that was historically only accessible to consumers with a lot of money or a lot of skill."[27]

This type of cultural arrogance is not just the bane of the for-profit industry—it can blind community colleges as well, leading them to potentially become "Netflixed" by other players such as private, for-profit institutions, career colleges, or even other community colleges that approach the industry in a different way.

For example, over a period of years, business and industry have found less and less value in the traditional academic measurement culture of Carnegie Units, grades, grade levels, and transcripts. Companies are growing weary of hiring individuals only to find that they do not possess sufficient knowledge, skills, abilities, or behaviors.

Increasingly, employers want to know if a graduate can perform specific skills. In early 2013, the Carnegie Commission (an organization whose proud traditions and distinguished history trace back to its 1905 founding by Andrew Carnegie and charter by an act of Congress a year later) announced that a study would be undertaken to consider possible flaws in the current credentialing system, and to explore other means of credentialing.

The results of this study were to have been released in early 2014, though did not appear until January 2015. This delay suggested, in my view, continuing concerns about how far the commission will go in recommending structural changes, attendant political pressures—to say nothing of cultural pressures in the academy to keep things the way they are. Certainly any significant departure from current practice would be met with skepticism and criticism, which also disincentivizes radical change.

Huge investments have been made in the current system: in lexicon, software designs, industry partnerships, contracts, registrar structures, articulation agreements, and more. To retrofit the entire ecosystem would cost billions for higher education institutions, and governments, as well as the businesses that support higher education, and political fervor would likely ensue. The process would take years to undertake and complete. Suffice it to say that there are many reasons—billions of reasons—why there is a bias to maintain the current structure.

When the report entitled "The Carnegie Unit: A Century-Old Standard in a Changing Education Landscape" was released by Carnegie Foundation for the Advancement of Teaching in 2015, even after a delay of over a year, it failed to produce or even suggest a new approach in the measurement of learning. The report rightfully acknowledges that there are many problems with the current system, which has existed for over a century, but the foundation is loath to suggest change. Rather, the report suggests that the current arrangement and structure (one originally based upon workload calculations and providing for pensions of teachers and their surviving spouses) are working and allow for new ideas and experimentation for the measuring of learning to occur. [28]

The Carnegie Unit is a poor proxy for measuring learning. We all know that, and we all complain about it, more so of late. Yet, given the opportunity to introduce a more meaningful tool, or innovative approach, the commission took a pass. The Carnegie group failed to respond to a quickening need for a better metric of student knowledge. Still, a few entrepreneurial organizations have stepped up to begin finding a suitable way to measure learning, and more will likely join them.

Not long after the initial announcement by the Carnegie Commission regarding its intention to study the credit hour, Southern New Hampshire University (SNHU), under the leadership of Paul J. LeBlanc, became one of the first institutions of higher education to offer online, regionally accredited degree programs built around workplace-defined competencies. In doing so, it successfully resolved the thorny issues of financial aid, direct assessment, credit hours, and related certifications, to the cheers of the private sector.

What has followed is a flurry of higher education activity around competency, mastery, and credentialing, with many colleges and universities playing catch-up. SNHU has redefined its mission and found a better way to serve the American workforce that is more accessible, affordable, and accountable. The university was recognized in 2014 as number twelve on the list of The World's Most Innovative Companies by Fast Company.

Other leading organizations such as the New American Foundation, the American Association of Community Colleges, and Western Governors University (WGU) are providing webinars and conferences designed to promote dialogue and professional development around this emerging field.

Of particular mention, WGU in late 2013 entered into a partnership with ten community colleges from across the country to advance shared learning around competency-based education (CBE). Sally M. Johnstone, WGU's vice president for academic advancement, is at the helm of this initiative, leveraging resources from the Bill and Melinda Gates Foundation, Carnegie, and others. Dr. Johnstone and WGU distribute their information widely, and particularly with community colleges, through articles, presentations, conferences, and collaboration.

In fall 2015, WGU expanded its partnership efforts and convened yet another conference, CBE4CC, designed to assist interested community colleges with competency-based education (CBE) work. Community college participants had a unique opportunity to learn from their colleagues about their journeys to solve some of the same institutional challenges associated with the implementation of CBE programs.

Their goal was to help other community colleges refine their planning and development around CBE. WGU also maintains a public website, www.CBEinfo.org, where visitors can learn about the experiences of the ten community colleges involved, the challenges they faced, and their successes over the past few years. Serving over 50,000 students per term across the United States, WGU is redefining higher education.

The long-held community college mission of serving the community with an open door should foster an environment that supports innovation. Yet, even when community college leaders are disposed to the idea, implacable challenges come in the form of cultural redefinition, as well as other unavoidable practicalities.

As one community college president phrased it at an association meeting, innovation is "the forbidden fruit"—meaning he wants to pursue it, but feels constrained by board policies, governmental interventions, union contracts, limited resources, and people issues.[29] Indeed, academic freedom policies and shared governance structures of community colleges present special considerations for the executive who pursues innovation. But we know that inaction has a predictable outcome.

STRENGTHENING ORGANIZATIONAL CULTURE

Advancing a creative culture is a tall order to be sure, and it must be continually supported and nurtured. To foster an organization's cultural development toward innovation, Frank Newman, Lara Couturier, and Jamie Scurry suggest routinely sharing information with college employees as to the institution's current relative success, or lack of success.[30]

Giving employees performance data to consider, as well as benchmarking data from other institutions, is an essential requirement for their understanding why change and ongoing innovation are necessary. Data sharing, when combined with national, state, and board expectations, may organically direct the conversation toward the need for change. The president must take great care not to assign blame for current underperformance to any one individual or group of individuals; otherwise, infighting and low morale may impede his or her ability to advance change.

Be advised that this dispersion of data itself might be disruptive to the organization, unless the college has already mandated focus on performance. The president and leadership team would do well to undertake this action only after developing a complete strategy for information delivery, including an appropriate narrative, key messaging points, and an outline for improvement with related timelines and deliverables.

Ideally, the president will lead the review and discussion of data, presenting it in an open light, clearly, succinctly, and within a broader regional context. Discussion must also include the rationale for noted variances, and possibly a discussion as to why the data are being shared now, not sooner or later.

This is a perfect time for the institutional leader to set the table for the scale and intensity of national catalysts including increasing accountabilities, accreditation, reduced resources, and the changed nature of the "social contract." Helping employees to understand and engage in the sense-making of this changed reality is vital, but it will take time.

Johansen notes that employees will be looking for both stability, continuity, and clarity in times of volatility, uncertainty, complexity, and ambiguity (VUCA). He explains that employees' work routine, up to the point of change, is what grounds them and provides clarity about what they do and why. In times of change, it's possible for them to lose clarity. Community college presidents can only advance their culture-of-innovation if they are clear about their intentions and the role for every employee within that vision.

CONCLUDING THOUGHTS ON CULTURE AND INNOVATION

The culture of today's community college is a formidable power that the president and other leaders must not only acknowledge, but understand and respect, before any type of transformation is possible. While working within the existing culture may be possible in some cases, the legacy work of an organization's leadership is the creation of a culture that embraces change and innovation.

Specifically, the president can develop clarity and undertake the redirection of the college's culture—a long-term proposition that necessitates advance preparation and understanding, including an assessment of marketplace dynamics and intentional innovation. The work also mandates an unwavering commitment from all parties involved—commitment to each other, to the process, and to the end goal.

Community college leadership must be ever mindful of the dynamic and changing nature of the environment, including realms beyond higher education. We cannot know the source of the next innovation. Keeping a keen eye to the horizon, remaining well-read, inquisitive, and open to new ideas, and pushing the boundaries are important innovation skills for community college leaders.

Without question, community colleges are not beyond becoming "Netflixed" by others—competitors who may not be invested in the open-access mission of our organizations, nor the traditions and lofty intentions of our work.

Do not underestimate the source of new innovations for the college, as they quite often can be generated from the talent already within. Creating the right culture within the college is important for those internal ideas to emerge and flourish. Creativity, risk taking, and allowances for potential failure are essential components of such a culture. Leadership is people.

NOTES

1. Kim S. Cameron and Robert E. Quinn, *Diagnosing and Changing Organizational Culture, Based on the Competing Values Framework* (San Francisco, CA: Jossey-Bass, 2011), 19.

2. Jim Collins, *Good to Great* (New York: HarperCollins Publishers, Inc., 2001).

3. Tom Kelley and Jonathan Littman, *The Art of Innovation: Lessons in Creativity from IDEO* (New York: Random House, 2001).

4. Steve Denning, "How Do You Change an Organizational Culture?" Forbes 21 (February 2014). Accessed November 11, 2014. http://www.forbes.com/sites/stevedenning/2011/07/23/how-do-you-change-an-organizational-culture/.

5. Rio Salado College, "Bill Gates Visits Rio Salado College." Accessed November 22, 2014. http://blog.riosalado.edu/2014/11/bill-gates-dr.html.

6. Chris Bustamante, personal communication to author, November 25, 2014.

7. Ibid.

8. Michael W. Kramer, *Organizational Socialization: Joining and Leaving Organizations* (Malden, MA: Polity Press, 2010).

9. Ibid., 18.

10. Collins, *Good to Great*.

11. Susan M. Heathfield, "20 Ways Zappos Reinforces Its Company Culture." *About Money*. Accessed January 3, 2015. http://humanresources.about.com/od/organizationalculture/a/how-zappos-reinforces-its-company-culture.htm.

12. Employee Benefit News, "Targeting Soft Skills Yields Hard Returns for Employers." Accessed December 15, 2014. http://ebn.benefitnews.com/news/zappos-hiring-practices-shrm-soft-skills-recruitment-2723282-1.html.

13. Meghan Biro, "The Onboarding Experience Matters to Your Future Employees." *Forbes* (June 2014). Accessed June 10, 2014. http://www.forbes.com/sites/meghanbiro/2014/06/01/the-onBoarding-experience-matters-to-your-future-employees/2/.

14. Cameron and Quinn, *Diagnosing and Changing Organizational Culture*.

15. Jay Rao and Joseph Weintraub, "How Innovative is Your Company's Culture?" *MIT Sloan Management Review*, 54 (2013): 29–37.

16. Waubonsee Community College, "Embracing Engagement Benefits Students, Community." Accessed November 26, 2014. http://www.waubonsee.edu/search/index.php?q=connect+collaborate.

17. Christine Sobek, personal communication to author, November 25, 2014.

18. *Chronicle of Higher Education*, "Great Colleges to Work For." Accessed June 6, 2014. http://chronicle.com/section/Great-Colleges-to-Work-For/156/.

19. Roger Connors and Tom Smith, *Change the Culture, Change the Game: The Breakthrough Strategy for Energizing Your Organization and Creating Accountability for Results* (New York: Penguin Group, 2011), 16–17.

20. Daniel J. Rowley, Herman D. Lujan, and Michael G. Dolence, *Strategic Change in Colleges and Universities: Planning to Survive and Prosper* (San Francisco, CA: Jossey-Bass Publishers, 1997).

21. Jackson College, "Statement of Beliefs." Accessed November 19, 2015. http://www.jccmi.edu/administration/president/MissionDocuments.htm.

22. John P. Kotter, *Leading Change* (Boston, MA: Harvard Business School Press, 1996), 156.

23. Connors and Smith, *Change the Culture, Change the Game: The Breakthrough strategy for Energizing Your Organization and Creating Accountability for Results*, 20.

24. Ibid.

25. Kotter, *Leading Change*.

26. Saul Kaplan, *The Business Model Innovation Factory: How to Stay Relevant When the World is Changing* (New York: John Wiley & Sons, 2012).

27. Clayton M. Christensen, "Disruptive Innovation." Accessed November 23, 2014. http://www.claytonchristensen.com/key-concepts/.

28. Carnegie Foundation for the Advancement of Teaching, "The Carnegie Unit: A Century-Old Standard in a Changing Education Landscape." 2015. Accessed February 1, 2015. http://www.carnegiefoundation.org/resources/publications/carnegie-unit/.

29. Michigan Community College Association, personal communication to author, July 22, 2013.

30. Frank Newman et al., *The Future of Higher Education: Rhetoric, Reality, and the Risks of the Market* (San Francisco, CA: Jossey-Bass, 2004).

FIVE

Assessment, Planning, and Innovation

"Without change there is no innovation, creativity, or incentive for improvement. Those who initiate change will have a better opportunity to manage the change that is inevitable."
— William Pollard

THE BUSINESS OF ENVIRONMENTAL ASSESSMENT

Higher education operates in a boundless ecosystem. However, as an industry, it has largely been confined by the walls of traditional methodologies, practices, and routines. As discussed in previous chapters, some of this constraint is borne of its own making through cultural norms, employee resistance, and leadership. Some is the result of a lack of foresight, structured observation, anticipation, prudence, and boldness.

Perhaps more compellingly, Christensen et al. noted that "disruptive innovation theory suggests the planning and business model of many traditional colleges and universities is broken. Their collapse is so fundamental that it cannot be stanched by improving the financial performance of endowment investments, tapping wealthy alumni donors more effectively, or collecting more tax dollars from the public. There needs to be a new model."[1]

However difficult to hear, I believe that this harsh appraisal is accurate. Community colleges repeatedly demonstrate tunnel vision and linear thinking about budgets, assessment, and planning methodologies, and the future in general. Even in the best cases, community colleges tend to compartmentalize innovation by creating an "idea drop box," or offering cash for ideas, rather than by accepting that innovation is comprehensive,

93

complex, fluid, and unique. Innovation must be integrated into everyday languages and processes.

Christensen suggests that higher education thoughtfully examine which innovations could be pursued by the organization to improve its position, and then determine which end of the market spectrum is the best place to begin.

Based upon their observation and research of industry experts Bill Gates, Andy Grove, and Steve Jobs, authors David Yoffie and Michael Cusumano concluded that before introducing new products or services, the first priority is to define the organization's unique value proposition to the consumer and its relative position in the marketplace. The organization's core competencies and competitive advantage must also be assessed.

Maintaining a unique competitive advantage is difficult for the long term, they assert, which is why they have found that leading strategists "build industry-wide platforms that bring together a broad ecosystem of partners engaged in complementary product and service innovation, as well as in related marketing, sales, service, and distribution."[2]

They recognize that it is difficult, at best, to determine from what direction change might come. Andy Grove, former Intel chief, and author of *Only the Paranoid Survive*, referred to the shifts that could fundamentally wreak havoc upon an organization as "10X changes":

> These 10X changes are both the biggest opportunities and the biggest threats any business can face. In some industries, they come every 20, 30, or even 100 years; in others, they can happen every five or ten years. Since 2007, for example, the smartphone and the tablet have launched typhoon-force winds through the communications and computer industries . . . the strategists' role is to identify and then devise strategies to handle these transformative periods. Recognizing a 10X change after the fact can be the kiss of death; recognizing it in time is a matter of awareness, timing, and preparation. As Grove notes, you have to act "when not everything is known, when the data aren't yet in. Even those who believe in a scientific approach to management will have to rely on instinct and personal judgement."[3]

As college leaders, we know, if we are honest with ourselves, that the more traditional tools for initiative selection and direction setting, including affinity diagrams; strengths, weaknesses, opportunities, and threats (SWOT) analyses; environmental scanning; decision trees; strategic planning; focus groups; and Gantt charts are only marginally effective in the pursuit of innovation.

Rather, these practices are largely extensions of the same methods that have been used for years to satisfy board, accrediting, governmental, and a multitude of other reporting requirements. Doesn't it stand to reason that if community colleges could forecast the next disruptive innovation using these techniques, they would have already capitalized on it? So why is our current approach to finding the future limited?

It is because innovation doesn't follow a process or system. It is often amorphous, organic, unstable, and sometimes serendipitous. Higher education, on the other hand, is risk-averse, often plodding, pedantic, and constrained, waiting for the supportive data, most of which are lagging indicators. Even the industry's most recent work with data analytics still falls short of providing the answers needed to engage innovative possibilities.

By the time we've formed our committees, considered the data, debated the issue, developed our plans, built the budget, gotten the necessary approvals, and mobilized, the opportunity has passed. Innovative and disruptive ideas don't present themselves in nicely gift-wrapped packages, perfectly timed to benefit your college. Actually, if change and innovation are not culturally encouraged and supported at your institution, the opportunities could be passing in front of you, without you seeing them.

Of course, there are a number of diviners who propose to do the work for you, suggesting what the future will likely hold based upon their observations and insights. These future projections of impact are largely extensions of what is currently known. For example, Jeff Selingo, editor at large for the *Chronicle of Higher Education*, suggests the following five areas as lasting disruptors of higher education:

- the higher education financial crisis;
- reduced state support;
- reduced numbers of students paying high tuition costs;
- availability of quality unbundled education alternatives; and
- higher education's declining value proposition.

Still other authors and prognosticators promote their own ideas about these issues, offering innovative solutions that range from massive open online courses (MOOCs), to courses delivered through XMRadio, to competency-based education (CBE), to spray-on solar cells that reduce heating costs, and other technologies. It's fairly risk-free to project near-future initiatives based upon what currently is, or what has recently been introduced into the environment. It's much harder to see the new and disruptive innovations coming. Few people, if any, anticipated the innovation and the impact on higher education from the Internet, tablets, LCD projectors, flat-panel technology, high fidelity medical simulation mannequins or social media platforms.

FINDING INNOVATION

What we find in the literature and through observation of other types of organizations is that there is no one, easy way to anticipate the next idea, nor predict its origin. There never has been. However, within innovative leaders is a commanding drive to improve, to think differently, to innovate, to challenge themselves, to thrive, and to take necessary risks.

Each of them has strong relational intelligence. They are disciplined, they strive for excellence rather than accepting mediocrity, they are incredibly hard workers, and they are expertly dedicated to their craft, almost to a fault. They are voracious readers and critical thinkers. They see relationships, intersections, critical paths, inflection points, and new dimensions that most others gloss over. They are experimenters, they are entrepreneurial, they fail, and they try again. They are open to new ideas, rejecting nothing out of hand. They contemplate multiple scenarios and futures from many sources, and are prepared to act upon any one of them in short order.

Consider the "Uberization" of higher education, for example. Uber is the world's largest cab company, comprised of "just-in-time" drivers who are unencumbered by many corporate challenges like fees, extensive licensing, dispatch routing, and payment equipment like fare calculators. Participating drivers use their own vehicles.

Uber owns not a single cab, and it doesn't define itself as a cab company, but rather as an international transportation network. It leverages an "on-demand sharing economy" through the use of smart phones, enabling consumers to access services and products with unused capacity at a reduced rate, a trend also known as "collaborative consumption."

Other examples of this sharing approach include NetJets, which provides access to air transportation on demand based on unused capacity; Expedia Hotels, which provides significant discounts to rooms based upon unused capacity in highly sought-after locations; SoundCloud, an Internet-based, common-spacing source for original music recording, uploading, and sharing and Capital Bikeshare, a company launched in 2008 in the metro DC area that makes bicycles readily available with over 350 pick-up and drop-off sites. And, as I was delighted to discover, the first thirty minutes are free. Couldn't the concept of excess capacity and an on-demand model extend to the way we serve students?

I believe the Uber concept could represent a significant disruption to the higher education industry. A *New York Times* article headline on January 28, 2015, read "Uber's Business Model Could Change Your Work." The article went on to say, "Just as Uber is doing for taxis, new technologies have the potential to chop up a broad array of traditional jobs into discrete tasks that can be assigned to people just when they are needed, with wages set by a dynamic measurement of supply and demand, and every worker's performance is constantly tracked, reviewed, and subject to the sometimes harsh light of customer satisfaction."[4]

Interestingly, there are an increasing number of relatively new organizations that are very comfortable with encouraging and posting customer experience reviews. For example, Airbnb, an excess-bed-capacity, accommodation-sharing community founded in 2008, provides in-home lodgings in over 190 countries worldwide, and records the experience of guests at hosting residences for other would-be couch travelers to consider in making their housing selections. By contrast, in higher education, we quake at the very idea of Rate My Professor, the College Scorecard, or other performance-based ratings.

Another example of an organization in the collaborative economy space, this one with clearer higher education linkages, is MentorPitch. Started in Dublin, Ireland, in 2014, MentorPitch is a cloud-based platform used for providing mentoring to universities and companies. For approximately seven hundred U.S. dollars a month, a network of over two thousand mentors worldwide will assist four hundred students.

According to founder Gerard Kiely, MentorPitch can provide open and private mentoring programs for alumni and employees alike. Each mentee is responsible for selecting his or her own mentor based upon mutual areas of interest. MentorPitch can also assist colleges in the development of their own structured, online mentoring programs, using the college's mentors who are accessible to students and employees. The company provides real-time data analytics and measurable outcomes to help the college determine the impact and effectiveness of the service.[5]

It's not a big innovation jump to apply the Uber on-demand, excess-capacity concept to higher education. Consider legal services, global online course aggregation and delivery, competency standards development, adjunct faculty sourcing, course development, student housing, and course placement writing assessments.

Assuming that there are provisions to ensure quality delivery, provider authenticity, and other certifications, many of these ideas could reduce costs and increasingly allow employees to concentrate their efforts on the value-added aspects of their work. Perhaps some of these excess support services could be obtained from other higher education institutions.

Consider also the development of education-based "boot camps" in which curriculum is based upon competencies derived from industry leaders. Gone are the traditional entrance requirements of ACT or SAT scores, high school GPA calculations, or service learning experiences. Boot camps seek only those who will work hard to earn the technical and interpersonal skills needed for employment at awaiting companies, many of which sponsor the camps, and even individual learners.

Limiting enrollments to fewer than two dozen students in two- to four-month programs, these camps charge about $1,000 per week to train students to write computer code. Other career- and vocation-based programs are under development from for-profit organizations and are largely a response to the fact that "trade schools [are] out of fashion, for-profit colleges [are] often dismissed as expensive dropout factories, and community colleges [are] failing to graduate a majority of their students."[6] Students can obtain jobs paying an average of $76,000, and up to $100,000, if they graduate from these highly selective boot camps.

The quest to become a well-rounded leader involves drawing upon unlikely sources and making creative connections. For example, what can we take away from the Apple Watch or iWatch? Can we apply this technology to the distribution of information, tuition payment strategies, instructional material review, or health assessment at the campus clinic or in nursing practice? Even before the wearable iWatch was released in early 2015, Penn State University announced a research initiative to consider its use as a learning tool in the classroom.[7]

Take the Oculus Rift, the virtual reality headset for 3D computer gaming. This innovation could be extended to engineering or health care where it might allow students to virtually walk through a heart, liver, or a nuclear reactor. Or think about Microsoft Cortana for Windows, the software-based digital assistant. Based on this technology, we might consider possibilities for improved employee efficiency, public interfaces to access college information, classroom assistance for students with disabilities, or automatic course scheduling. Even advancements that seem unrelated can be framed, altered, or repurposed to serve our needs, or at least be used to fuel the curiosity that drives innovation.

These are just a small sampling of innovative solutions that have been placed before us by start-ups, entrepreneurs, and visionaries, and I present them to encourage college leaders to look to the environmental fringes where more than just the obvious ideas exist. Think forward using multiple scenarios, debate ideas—challenge assumptions, think kaleidoscopically, and talk with leaders in industries other than your own. Read publications outside your field or particular interest area. For example, read *Motor Trend, Aviation Technology, Entrepreneur, Latin Trade, Lego Magazine, Discover, Science, Electronic Design, ArtAsiaPacific, Cooking Light, Dwell, Smithsonian, Health, Ebony,* and *Sky & Telescope.* There is great advantage in learning the latest in other industries and fields. The future could come around any corner.

MENTAL MINECRAFT

One of the tools often used by innovation prospectors looking to advantage their organization, or minimally, to remain competitive, is scenario planning, or what I often call, "Mental Minecraft." Its namesake, the popular Microsoft game (Minecraft) is a virtual, limitless, creative, innovative and adventuresome space. Players use scores of building blocks, actively breaking, constructing, altering, or moving blocks around to create new designs, new communities, and new realms.

Mental Minecraft not only allows the creator to develop, but also to test his or her ideas and to study their workability and defensibility in changing environmental conditions, and with various nocturnal creatures lurking about. Mental Minecraft can be an interesting tool for higher education leaders as well.

For example, consider the following present state and a plausible future scenario for community colleges. Historically and still today, community colleges collaborate. They are largely not competitors with each other. Rather, we behave more like Andy Grove's notion of a "platform." We freely share information about how we face common challenges, and through conferences, workshops, webinars, and books like this one, we provide detailed strategies for our most promising or proven practices.

But considering the declining commitment and resources from the federal and state government, as well as from local taxpayers, especially when combined with declining numbers of students, community colleges will, over time, have to compete. Increasingly, we will find competitive advantage in keeping ideas and innovations to ourselves as long as possible and to the extent that we can as a public entity. How long we remain public institutions is largely a question of how long we can deliver upon our value proposition for taxpayers.

In truth, we are already on this path. Consider the broad, multistate, and international delivery of online courses. Consider also groups of community colleges that provide national and international training contracts in the backyard of other community college districts, as in the case of Global Corporate College.

Rising competition will likely cause traditionally respected boundaries, such as county lines, school districts, and state and national borders, to be negated. Increasingly, neither students nor technology will recognize this antiquated compartmentalization. Private and for-profit higher education have exposed our market delivery shortcomings and are exploiting them through broad market penetration, aggressive recruitment methods, sophisticated customer-focused systems, shrewd business acumen, and political prowess.

At some point we will conclude that we are no longer able to feed the current business and operational model. Standard activities such as reverse transfer, dual enrollment, international recruitment, block transfer, and dual admissions only delay the inevitable. In some ways, even our current work on the "student success completion agenda" is a nod to the need for change based upon marketplace competition.

On some level we recognize that it is easier, and less expensive, to retain students who are currently enrolled, versus chasing new students. The same conclusion was reached by professionals in economic development in the 1980s. It was easier to support existing businesses in the community or state than to continue the so-called "smokestack chasing."

Other industries like health care, secondary education, and nonprofits, will meet this future as well. Perhaps our solution will be to close smaller community colleges and merge to create larger districts: mega–community colleges. Some would argue that institutions such as Miami Dade College, Dallas County Community College, Los Angeles Community College, and Maricopa Community College are already mega–community colleges. It may be possible to extend this mega concept to create large rural community college districts as well.

The competitive community college and the mega–community college are hard scenarios to consider, to be sure. Once you moved past the initial shock value of the scenario, what were your thoughts about how best to position your organization for this possible reality? Did you simply scoff at the notion and move on, or did you consider its implications fully for your community college? If the latter did it bring to mind current areas of exposure for your institution? Did it prompt you to consider what you might do differently in order to hedge your bet on this particular scenario?

Regardless of your answers, this type of Mental Minecraft represents a process that boards of trustees, presidents, and other community college leaders must regularly practice in order to best capitalize upon, or prepare for, possible changes in the not-too-distant future.

In his book *What Excellent Community Colleges Do*, Josh Wyner, executive director of the College Excellence Program for the Aspen Institute, reviews community colleges that have advanced through the Aspen Prize process, to glean implications for the future. He notes that

> there is an explosion in the competition for students traditionally served by community colleges. New schools, many of them for-profit endeavors, bring substantial investment capital, well-developed marketing strategies, and new ways of thinking about educational delivery."[8]

> Unencumbered by tradition, these [for-profit] schools are reinventing faculty roles, measurement of student learning, and program structures and schedules in ways that are not so easy for traditional community colleges to emulate.[9]

These competitive institutions move with alacrity. They are unfettered by bureaucracy, unconstrained by ritual, unrestricted in their physical or virtual deployment, and rapid in response. This competitive threat is metaphorically right off the bow, and I'm afraid there will be no avoiding the collision. Still, there are many strategies that community colleges can execute to counter the actions of competitors, if we are creative enough and have the courage to forge ahead.

THINKING DIFFERENT, DIMENSIONALLY AND OPPORTUNISTICALLY

As community college leaders, it is preferable to be on the front end of innovation, and to anticipate and prepare for new competitive forces, rather than to just react to them. To do so requires attention to our changing environment. It also requires embracing present-day challenges as opportunities to innovate, improve relevance, enhance student and organizational success, and stave off competition.

One particular response strategy for existing problems could be stronger vertical integration with other educational institutions. As an example, Ken Ender, president of William Raney Harper College, located in the greater Chicago metro area, sought a different method to address the developmental education needs of incoming freshmen.

Rather than increasing the number of courses required for developmental students, and blaming K–12 schools for not adequately preparing them, President Ender approached the superintendents of the three primary feeder high schools in his district with a simple question. How can we better integrate our work to ensure that high school graduates are ready for college?

This approach elicited a positive reaction from the superintendents, who began meeting regularly with Ender and their respective staffs. This cross-district team assessed the broader educational environment and pored over the data, which indicated that the majority of incoming community college students tested into developmental math.

Their investigation revealed a disconnect between the competencies taught in high school Algebra II courses in each district and the competencies expected by Harper College. The faculty and teachers subsequently worked together to align Algebra II with the college's highest level developmental math courses, and they created a course to bridge the gap. High school students who tested as noncollege ready in their junior year were encouraged to take the new course in their senior year.

These efforts resulted in a 27 percent increase in college-level math enrollment by recent high school graduates over a period of five years. Harper College evaluated the problem from its own perspective, but the college found success by working with local schools instead of spurring conflict with them.

What's more, President Ender told me that they are so committed to this work, and concerned about developmental education costs detracting from limited Pell funding, that the college has developed what they call the Harper Promise Program. This initiative creates incentives for high school students to meet annual benchmarks to ensure that they are college ready when they graduate. If they achieve the benchmarks, they earn up to four free semesters at Harper College. Specifically, students must maintain at least a 2.0 GPA in high school, graduate on time, and perform similarly while at Harper College. [10]

The college's board put $5 million into a fund to launch the Harper Promise Program, and its foundation board has committed to raise an additional 5 million. The three area high school superintendents also actively support and assist in the fundraising effort. A separate nonprofit organization, the Northwest Educational Council for Student Success (NECSS), was subsequently established to formalize the partnership between the college and the three school districts. The institutions are currently working on aligning levels of English as well. [11]

Words and ideas are not enough for innovative leaders. They must jump into the thick of things and be trusted to get things done. Whether by fundraising millions of dollars to improve success rates for developmental students, having difficult conversations with unlikely partners, leveraging personal integrity to build relationships, or taking a leap of faith in an effort to solve a problem, institutional leaders, at all levels in our community colleges, are always assessing their environment, thinking in new dimensions, and considering options. They are action oriented to facilitate change.

In some cases, innovative response strategies to competitive forces may involve changing the products or services you provide. Take Lake Michigan College (LMC), for example, located in Benton Harbor, Michigan, which never had student housing on campus since its founding in 1946.

Based upon market demographics, student demand, and increasing competition, President Robert Harrison and the LMC board of trustees decided to add a facility to house nearly two hundred residents in the fall semester of 2014. As projected, this initiative provided additional revenue for the college. This enterprise was also disruptive to the college insofar as having students living on campus mandated operational change. For example, LMC had to hire residence life staff and provide security for students who would be on campus overnight and on weekends. They also needed to contemplate issues such as student in-room safety, meal options, and facility maintenance.

The action was also a risk in that the college had no prior experience with student housing, and it had no significant level of debt on its books. Before LMC's addition of student housing, only six of Michigan's twenty-eight public community colleges had introduced the student housing option. The availability of housing, typical to four-year colleges, is becoming more popular at the community college level. Nationally, about 25 percent of community colleges currently offer student housing. [12]

In many midwestern states, nearly all community colleges have student housing, though in some cases it is managed by a third party. LMC's experience was clearly an innovative step for the college. It was an attempt to remain competitive since a neighboring community college and university offered student housing.

In the consideration of innovation or competitive response strategies, such as commencing new initiatives like student housing, the assessment of risk and the capacity for risk are important considerations for trustees, presidents, and institutional leaders alike.

ASSESSMENT OF INSTITUTIONAL RISK TOLERANCE

Community college leaders who have successfully introduced innovation on their campuses have a strong sense of their organization's capacity for innovation. Despite their underlying awareness of the urgency for change, these leaders also understand the importance of timing. They consider the degree of stress, outcome variability, and the current workload of personnel. Equally important, they have an intuitive grasp on what employees are able and willing to withstand over a sustained period of time.

More than three decades ago, international management consultant Peter Drucker observed, "The one certainty about tomorrow is that it will be a time of turbulence. And in turbulent times, the first task of management is to make sure of the institution's capacity for survival, to make sure of its structural strength, and soundness, of its capacity to survive a blow, to adapt to sudden change, and to avail itself of new opportunities." [13] This assessment is as resonant today as it was then.

In the breakneck pace of the present day, which is bracketed by increasing demands from students, parents, legislators, and others, as presidents we find ourselves wondering if it is possible to be a comprehensive community college any longer, let alone to be "all things to all people." Constantly responding to emerging issues and opportunities is time consuming, taxing, and, in many ways, distracting.

The community college president must be able to sift through the college's many available options and evaluate every stimulus in terms of its relevance to the college's mission and vision and impact upon staff and operations, all while simultaneously evaluating the environment that these possibilities would create.

The risk-reward determination for each community college president will be different because each college is different, so contexts, resources, threats, and opportunities are also different. Each college's assessment will involve part art, and part science. The art is the use of experience from previous successes and failures to guide future action. The art also includes the president's knowledge of his or her institution and its people, and their capacities, all of which is explored in the next section.

The science of risk assessment involves quantifiable elements such as dollars to be invested, time required, the magnitude of the project, and the project's alignment with institutional vision and goals. The scientific determination should also include an appraisal of the opportunity cost, including the cost over time of declining the proposed initiative.

Alternatively, if the project is pursued, what is the opportunity cost for not reserving resources for another, better opportunity, or a more significant threat that might emerge? Again, what is that cost over time? Even after the art and science determinations are made, and the political landscape is considered, the selection of an initiative comes down to an assessment of your own tolerance for risk, as well as your fortitude in pressing on. Sometimes, despite the data, the decision comes down to a gut feeling. This is not a very technical component of the decision-making process, but over the years, I have found that inner voice worth heeding.

THE IMPORTANCE OF PLANNING

When all the facets of innovation and its implications have been considered and addressed, a sound plan must follow. Too often, however, this critical step is poorly executed. John Kotter suggests three reasons why.

First, given the fact that community colleges effectively live in "dog years," employees often feel overwhelmed by the urgency and speed with which new plans must be implemented, and therefore may not buy into the vision early on. Additionally, he notes that when pressed for time, and under significant pressure, employees tend to plan poorly, plan less, or not plan at all because they are too busy doing the essential work of the day.

Second, employees often seem unable to reconcile the perceived, or even practical, conflict that comes with maintaining their current workload and simultaneously advancing a new initiative.

Third, often there is a lack of commitment from the managers who are advancing the innovation, or an insufficient number of managers in the first place, so employees are left feeling directionless. As Kotter says, "With no sense of urgency, a lack of key managers on the guiding coalition, the failure to communicate an effective vision well, and little effort put into broad-based employee empowerment, people in overmanaged and underled organizations sit on the sidelines during change, especially managers who could be instrumental in producing needed short-term results."[14]

You may be able to forego proper planning, and planning strategies, and let fate determine the vision and outcomes for an organization, but given the limited resources available to higher education combined with increasing levels of accountability, it would be not only foolish—it would be irresponsible.

There is a variety of planning schema for a complete innovation plan, but each generally involves environmental assessment; definition of objectives, strategy, and end goals; consideration of alternatives; discussions about resource allocation; creation of a timeline; and a post-hoc evaluation.

The overarching structure and development methodology is the responsibility of the president, with counsel from the board. One successful schema is based upon author John Kotter's research of successful companies. He translated his rich observations into eight sequential steps for meaningful and transformative change, and he urges that the steps be followed in precise order so as to avoid some of the problems encountered by companies in his study:

1. *Establishing a Sense of Urgency*—Assess the environment and market and consider both potential and actual crises and opportunities;
2. *Creating the Guiding Coalition*—Establish a core team capable of assisting leadership in advancing change;
3. *Developing a Vision and Strategy*—Define a clear vision to help set institutional direction as well as strategies to realize it;
4. *Communicating the Change Vision*—Communicate the new vision, rationale, achievement strategies, and the role of the Guiding Coalition frequently, and through multiple channels;
5. *Empowering Broad-Based Action*—Remove obstacles, systems and structures that undermine the new vision, and encourage risk taking, unique ideas, and action;
6. *Generating Short-Term Wins*—Provide early, visible improvements and victories, recognizing and rewarding those directly involved;
7. *Consolidating Gains and Producing More Change*—Leverage increased credibility from early successes to change structures and policies that don't match the transformational agenda. Employ, promote, and develop those persons who can implement the change agenda; and
8. *Anchoring New Approaches in the Culture*—Advance improved performance and vision-aligned behavior through more and better leadership and management, articulating connections between new behaviors and success of the organization.[15]

In a survey of ninety-two organizational leaders from fourteen public and fourteen private-sector organizations, Mike Doyle, Tim Claydon, and Dave Buchanan concluded that certain core elements of planning are necessary for organizational change to occur, based upon gaps that often arrest the change process. These components are as follows:

1. Manage the number of initiatives undertaken;
2. Establish visible preplanning and assessment systems;

3. Support employees with the stressful elements of change;
4. Provide critical, focused organizational communications with employees;
5. Establish the means for appreciating individual and organizational learning from the change process;
6. Ensure inclusion of strategies that build commitment, trust, and engagement in the process; and
7. Provide ongoing change-management professional development to employees.[16]

Ultimately, the president is the responsible party for the plan and its implementation. That said, often one of the struggles leaders face with such extensive employee involvement is finding the optimum juncture between ensuring the achievement of goals and objectives and engaging employees fully in the process of planning for the future.

Intel's Andy Grove, for example, reports having grappled with finding the right mix of engagement, autonomy, and leadership in others, with needing to focus solely on getting the job done the way his vision prescribed it. He directed middle managers to plan and make resource decisions, believing this strategy would generate early buy-in and commitment to the work.

Initially, this process worked, but over time, Grove found that expanded, inclusive, "bottom-up" planning did not result in the speed necessary to affect change in their highly competitive marketplace. He also concluded that due to the narrowness of employee experience, their limited perspective regarding broad company issues, and their inability to make hard decisions, executive and senior management was in a better position to conduct the planning.[17]

Nevertheless, leaders cannot ignore personnel in the planning phase. Collaboration is essential. Ideally, a core planning team should be utilized, one that is limited in size and comprised of individuals who possess appropriate knowledge, experience, skills, and commitment to the initiative.

The leader should also consider the value of including people both internal and external to the organization. The president must explain the planned innovation in all its depth, and invite comment thereafter. The more that the plan is evaluated, debated, and refined on the front end, the better the likelihood of its success. However, leaders must be careful to avoid extensively directing or micromanaging the process.

Richard Rhodes, president of Austin Community College (ACC) in Texas, consistently demonstrates the value of involving employees in the identification of persistent problems, and in seeking solutions to resolve them. Like most community colleges, ACC grappled with students not persisting from developmental education courses to college-level courses, particularly in the area of mathematics.

The college had worked with the Achieving the Dream (ATD) organization and expert consultants, and they had incorporated the improvement of student success in developmental education courses into the organization's Quality Enhancement Plan (QEP). Still, President Rhodes concluded that they were not achieving a significant level of meaningful difference.

Understanding that the math faculty were central to any discussion about a new and innovative solution for improved student success, he invited them to help redesign the work. A committee was appointed and worked to review QEP feedback, ATD program feedback, and other institutional data.

The group concluded that they needed to prepare students for an Algebra II pathway, as part of the college's focus on science, technology, engineering, and math programs (STEM). Considering a model used at Virginia Tech as a basis for design, Rhodes sent teams of math faculty to multiple institutions to seek out promising practices.

Upon their return, the committee synthesized their ideas and anecdotes and proposed a plan that would suit ACC. The idea of the ACCelerator was born, but administration knew it would be a substantial undertaking if it was to have the level of impact they hoped to achieve. To that end, with the support of the board, the president and his leadership team made a bold move and acquired property at a former shopping mall to bring the innovative plan to reality.

In the fall of 2014, the 32,000-square-foot building reopened, having been transformed into a high-tech learning facility with fifteen study rooms and 604 virtual desktop computer stations that provided individualized, self-paced learning. The computers used Aleks software, and developmental math students were required to utilize the ACCelerator a minimum of nine hours per week, which was monitored by the system itself. Students could also access the software remotely, including from their own homes.

In addition to technology-based instruction, the ACCelerator featured an extensive support network of faculty, counselors, advisors, tutors, librarians and other staff members, all ready to help students succeed. Classrooms and study rooms surrounded the clusters of computer stations.

In the first semester alone, over seven hundred students used the ACCelerator. Before the creation of the ACCelerator, the term-to-term attrition rate of developmental education students at ACC was between 30 to 35 percent. However, after the first semester that figure fell to 7.5 percent. What's more, 43 percent of the students using the center earned the equivalent of 1.5 grade levels in their studies. Some students reportedly moved through three semesters of material in as little as seven weeks.

In conversation, President Rhodes shared some hesitation and concern about the innovation from the onset. A few employees complained that there were no blueprints for this idea because there was no one else in the field doing this kind of work, let alone on this scale. Others scoffed that the location was ill-suited for the college because the area was in economic decay. President Rhodes persisted. After the center opened, one of the faculty members who initially expressed concern about the idea told him that it was exactly the type of work the college should be doing.

When I asked President Rhodes about the key reasons for the success of this initiative, he noted three: 1) Creating and incorporating a great deal of data into the process; 2) Engaging those working in the developmental mathematics area, as well as those who would be involved in the project, and asking them to consider other models in their planning; and 3) Providing strong committee support by the president and administration in the process.

He described ACC's work as evolving, yet the college already has other instructional divisions asking to be a part of the ACCelerator. And, as icing on the cake, the area surrounding the former mall is now experiencing an economic renewal by virtue of the college's acquisition and investment in the former shopping mall.[18] Clearly, looking to the horizon, paying attention to what's working elsewhere, making solid plans, and meaningfully engaging employees in the work have the potential to yield amazing results.

Like Rhodes, President Christine Sobek of Waubonsee Community College (WCC) in Illinois recognizes the importance of employee involvement in the innovative planning process. For example, President Sobek undertakes an annual Vision Project that projects twenty to thirty years into the future. The college uses a variety of internal and external meetings to gather the perspectives of employees, students, and community members as it reviews its mission documents and achievements in relation to the constantly changing community college environment.

Dr. Sobek and her leadership team are constantly scanning the environment. They are voracious readers and actively engaged in professional conferences and state-level initiatives. In fact, all administrators at WCC are encouraged to serve on various community boards and committees. Ultimately, the Vision Project results in a projection of the college into the future with multiple markers to guide their path.[19]

Other types of plans utilized by community colleges are built around a more abbreviated planning process. Where the broad-reaching plans tend to be less definitive due to their distant-future projections, the short-term plans tend to be more specific. Some colleges employ a continuous planning methodology wherein plans are reviewed multiple times each year.

This particular strategy allows for ongoing reevaluation of the environment and reassessment of goals, with adjustments as needed. Generally speaking, the shorter a plan becomes in the overall time horizon, the more it tends to be operational in nature, providing greater clarity around outcomes and resource implications.

As with other components of higher education, we can take cues about planning from outside of our industry. Mary Jo Haddad, former CEO of the Hospital for Sick Children (SickKids), based in Toronto, engaged the Innosight consulting organization to develop an elegant and straightforward system for advancing innovation.

The system has three principal elements: 1) Creation of an Innovation Blueprint—this document outlines the type of innovations the hospital intends to pursue, as well as the demand for them, and rationale to support the choices. This component often involves focus groups of employees and others to explore ideas further; 2) Development of an Innovation Pipeline—this element codifies specific requirements and resources necessary to make the innovation a reality. This process also includes the use of a "Central Innovation Group" at the hospital that considers innovations, prioritizes them, advances them, and brings them to scale; and 3) Development of an Innovative Culture—this last stage addresses Jim Collins' notion of having the right people in the right seats on the bus of innovation.

This strategic planning process at SickKids has been credited with transforming the organization and enhancing its ability to serve its patients.[20] As a result of this planning design, the quality of pediatric care has improved along a number of metrics. It has expanded its network of services to include other community hospitals and the community itself, as well as other off-site locations.

Michael Apkon, CEO, has continued the innovative approach by utilizing an abbreviated planning tool to get input from the young patients, as well as from parents, employees, and health officials. One result is an initiative called Project Horizon. The project is designed to integrate the pediatric healthcare system in the region with the particular goal of delivering high-quality, specialized pediatric care through investments in technology and infrastructure.[21]

The key takeaway on planning for innovation is that the longer period of time encompassed by the plan, the less likely the institution will be able to institute significant innovation. This is true primarily because by the time a college arrives at the intended time to implement the change or innovation, years after its planning commenced, it is highly unlikely that the idea itself will still be innovative. It follows to question whether it is even possible to plan for innovation. The short answer is yes. To provide additional context and examples, a more detailed planning approach for innovation is explored a few pages hence.

If a college can successfully deploy action strategies, while simultaneously adjusting organizational culture and adapting its planning as it advances, then it will be well positioned to arrive at the intended destination. A college's leaders may wish to include supportive planning elements, such as regular listening tours with the college's internal and external communities, employee collaboration similar to that utilized at WCC, and win/win or interest-based bargaining (IBB). These and other methods can be important tools for college planning.

INNOVATION, PLANS, AND ADAPTABILITY

Planning is a conceit. Significant work and resources go into the creation of a planning document, and amid celebration and relief, we conclude the effort happy in the knowledge that we know where we are going. No plan is that good. Some might even argue that the plan is outmoded the moment it is printed. When the winds of change blow, we are often impacted by unpredicted factors, those pesky challenges or unique opportunities that did not make it into our plan, or those that take us totally by surprise.

Therefore, community college leaders need to be nimble, able to tack or jibe the sailboat quickly in response to unexpected changes in the prevailing wind. Necessary skills for leaders include flexibility, adaptability, agility, and the ability to embrace ambiguity. A leader does not have the luxury to remain intransigent in his or her direction, regardless of what the plan says. No plan should be a straightjacket for the future. Otherwise, at best, you pass on the opportunity for additional gains that you could not conceive at the time, and, at worst, you encounter problems that can further disadvantage your organization.

One example of unpredicted change on the community college scene was the year-round availability of Pell grants in 2010. Had colleges had sufficient forewarning of its coming, they could have aggressively positioned their institutions with media campaigns and recruitment strategies, as well as school and employer visits, to leverage the summer grant opportunity.

A year later, the winds changed again, and Summer Pell was gone, so colleges again needed to adapt. Unanticipated cost overruns, implementation problems, and abuse by some institutions brought a worthwhile and promising imitative to an abrupt end. As a postscript, there remains some hope for year-round availability of Pell grants in the reauthorization of the Higher Education Act (HEA) of 1965, though this is an opportunity that we cannot know, or plan for.

The Pell grant is only one example of unanticipated change. There are a host of others. For example, a change in state law might alter state aid support distribution based upon the achievement of defined outputs. The local millage support you've had for the past century could be unexpectedly defeated in a ballot tax renewal request. A million-dollar gift from the estate of a recently deceased alumna may appear. A new trustee who ran on a platform of reform could be elected. Or maybe a peer institution wishes to partner with your community college to advance a competency-based initiative. The point here is that where the future is concerned, especially where it involves politics, little is certain, and colleges who wish to innovate must learn to respond opportunistically.

One strategy is to consider each opportunity that presents itself, on its own merit. At Rio Salado Community College, President Bustamante considers unexpected change relative to its alignment with the direction of the college. He feels that the college has a solid operational and instructional foundation to build upon, for the right opportunity.

He is clear about the college's core mission, strengths, and resource availability, noting that "complication, high costs, and the nature of potential partners involved can take away from our focus and we need to be careful about that." [22] He weighs every new idea carefully against the fact that the institution's plate is already pretty full. He is judicious in his selection process, as well he, and every leader, should be.

As an alternative to the individual consideration of each idea as it emerges, I propose an option that incorporates flexibility into a shorter time frame. I find that most opportunities for change and innovation do not come looking for us, though for large and well-resourced community colleges with strong reputations, they very well may.

In fact, I am often intrigued by the regularity with which metropolitan colleges with strong leaders, including League for Innovation in the Community College institutions, are able to secure grants and partner on cutting-edge opportunities, and then be recognized for these achievements. But the bulk of our nation's community colleges are smaller, suburban or rural, and they operate with severely limited resources.

Perhaps these colleges have an advantage in being a little more nimble. They may be able to respond more quickly to an opportunity than their more prosperous counterparts. A proactive strategy is essential in their case, especially in regard to internal opportunities. Many employees at these smaller colleges stand ready to present innovative ideas. They just need a pathway, one with less bureaucracy and more support, to activate their good ideas.

Acting upon innovation requires a set of decision criteria for evaluation, space within your college (mental and physical) for growth, and an approach that incentivizes openness to the opportunities for change, regardless of their origin. Scott Anthony, David Duncan, and Pontus Siren, based upon their considerable research, note that most organizations complicate this approach and remain haphazard in their plan for innovation:

Few [advance innovation] in an orderly, reliable way. In far too many organizations, the big breakthroughs happen despite the [organization]. Successful innovations typically follow invisible development paths and require acts of individual heroism or a heavy dose of serendipity. Successive efforts to jump-start innovation through, say, hack-a-thons, cash prizes for inventive concepts, and on-again, off-again task forces frequently prove fruitless. Great ideas remain captive in the heads of employees, innovation initiatives take way too long, and the ideas that are developed are not necessarily the best efforts or the best with strategic priorities. [23]

The authors recommend the creation of a "minimum variable innovation system" (MVIS) to formally drive innovation. MVIS is designed to encourage the generation of ideas and to advance the ideas that are likely to succeed. Central to this approach is support from the organization's leaders. The system, which the authors argue can be formalized in as few as ninety days, is based upon four steps:

1. Classify innovations as either disruptive or sustaining and determine where gaps may currently exist between organizational goals and current operations;
2. Target specific areas of strategic opportunity through conversations with customers and employees;
3. Establish an innovation team committed to advancing the organization through change, creating a process checklist to ensure that they fully consider and vet each idea; and
4. Develop a means to provide ongoing support to the MVIS team and the advancement of innovative ideas. [24]

Regardless of the process used, intentionality is the most important component of advancing change in the community college, and it is essential that internal and external communities perceive and appreciate this intention.

SANDBOX-BUILDING 101:
CONSIDERING THE INNOVATION TO PURSUE

The first and best place to determine which change or innovation should be pursued is within your college. Several community colleges have historically demonstrated the value of this selection process. Sinclair Community College in Ohio, Montgomery Community College in Pennsylvania, and Austin Community College in Texas are examples of organizations that have allowed for more than a contingency line in their operational budgets for investment in strategic opportunities. They have created a space for innovation to occur without undue risk, a place where employees can experiment, play and, yes, fail, in the quest to improve the organization. This space is what I like to call a "sandbox."

What is a sandbox exactly? A sandbox can be chronological, as in the case of 3M, which allocates work time to each employee for innovation consideration, as long as it is related to the employee's field or the general advancement of the organization. A sandbox can be cultural. Part of the ethos of the organization, part of its lore and aura, is engrained in the way it does things. A sandbox can be physical, a laboratory of sorts, as is the case at Bergen Community College, where its Center for Innovation in Teaching and Learning allows faculty and staff to explore sundry instructional technologies and promising practices.[25] This type of space typically includes computer equipment, library resources, software, collaboration-type furniture, lots of whiteboard space, and coffee. These innovation sandboxes may or may not be staffed.

Another example is Renton Technical College in Renton, Washington, one of a handful of community colleges that has taken the physical sandbox one step further. They created an Office of Research and Development with administrative and staff support. This space is accessible to all college employees, administrators, faculty, students, and the community. It is used primarily to enhance planning and institutional decision making. The office also provides support for grant writing, survey deployment, strategic planning, and research.

Sandboxes can be virtual and incorporate collaboration software such as Google Docs, SharePoint, Dabbleboard, or Thinkature with video communications like FaceTime, Skype, GoToMeeting, Adobe Connect, ooVoo Pro, or other web-based HD conferencing software. Relatedly, colleges can provide distance-learning sandbox labs, which are well suited for faculty who teach online courses. These might include support equipment like LCD projection systems, access to the college's course management system (CMS), and computers and development software for course creation.

Finally, a sandbox can exist ideologically and can be established anywhere by following a process model. Central New Mexico Community College in Albuquerque created a process called FRIES: Focus, Research, Implement, Evaluate, and Synthesize. This methodology continuously generates innovations from employees, keeping multiple initiatives in play concurrently, each with a unique timeline. One such FRIES project resulted in the CNM STEMulus Center, which assists entrepreneurs, businesses, government agencies, and others with developing relevant economic innovations in the community.

The above organizations have demonstrated the courage to create stimulating, supportive, and entrepreneurial space for innovation to occur, accepting all of the messy bits that come with it, including failure. Providing a practical environment that supports innovation by extension supports the pursuit of cultural redirection that is necessary for address-

ing the changing dynamic of the community college in a globally competitive environment.

If community colleges are going to be effective in the long term, I
believe it will be, in part, because presidents and their boards have invested in sandboxes where employees can bring forward their unique
experiences and ideas in the hopes of better serving students, their department, the college, and the community.

INITIATIVE SELECTION

The inevitable variety of innovation can be a positive thing. There is great
institutional benefit to diversity of thought, ideation, and creativity. The
accumulation of ideas from many sources—including those imposed by
law, competition, or a donor, but especially those deriving from the community—can build buy-in and commitment. This reality should influence
the president to treat the source of ideas with equal regard, regardless of
whether the ideas are intentionally sought or unsolicited. We must avoid
the "not-invented-here" bias and remain open-minded to ideas from outside our institutions.

Many of the ideas, creative solutions, and new strategies that come
before college leaders could probably find a home in the breadth of their
mission and vision statements, perhaps even in their strategic plans. But
not all of them should be—nor can be—pursued, so which ones win out?
While important, congruence with the college's mission documents cannot be the sole metric by which such determinations are made.

As president of Apple Inc., Steve Jobs said "no" to innovation, projects, and ideas about what Apple should do next far more times than he
said "yes." Jobs once remarked that just because you can do something
doesn't necessarily mean you should.[26] As the head of a multinational,
multi-billion-dollar corporation, with his hands on seemingly unlimited
resources, Jobs had to be a "sifter." He chose only those projects that
would be of the highest benefit for the resources invested (i.e., people,
finances, facilities, and information), and he would not be distracted from
his vision for the company. He also possessed a keen understanding of
organizational capacity, and the number of projects that could be worked
on simultaneously and efficaciously. Community college presidents must
do the same.

Colleges with proven success in selecting innovative initiatives characteristically demonstrate alignment between intended action and stated
organizational priorities. For example, Kirkwood Community College
(KCC) in Cedar Rapids, Iowa, had a culinary and hospitality arts program like many other community colleges across the country. KCC
sought to position itself in a market space untapped by any other community college. It undertook the construction of a full-service hotel that

not only provides a practical education for students in the culinary and hospitality management industry, but also generates a profit for the college. More than a hotel, it is also an active teaching facility.

The commitment of the hotel is to provide guests with a high-quality experience through a one-to-one employee-to-guest ratio. As part of the overall guest experience, the hotel sports first-rate rooms and open spaces, and offers guests wines that are made at the college. According to Mick Starcevich, president of KCC, students who study culinary arts and baking, or hotel/motel/restaurant management, have firsthand experiences in the delivery of service and event management for crowds of up to six hundred people in the hotel conference center.

In fiscal year 2014, the conference center held forty-eight weddings and wedding receptions. The proof of the program's success exists not only in revenues, but also through its many regional and national awards for excellence in hospitality. Starcevich added that the hotel is rated at the Four Diamonds level (an industry standard of quality) and, as such, is one of only two hotels of this caliber in the entire state of Iowa (there are no Five Diamond ratings), which is truly an achievement.[27] KCC had no template to follow, as is often the case when working in innovation space. But this example demonstrates what is possible when a college demonstrates risk taking, boldness, and skill in seeking innovations that are consistent with its mission and advance college priorities.

FORMULATION OF A COMMUNICATIONS STRATEGY

"VUCA" is an acronym popularized by the military that stands for volatility, uncertainty, complexity, and ambiguity. Community college leaders operate within environments that are replete with VUCA. The development, articulation, and communication of a project plan is essential for success in leading change. As part of early project communication, the leader must pay special attention to the "stage crafting," that is, laying the groundwork and time frame. Poorly managed communication can sink any initiative at the early stages of the process.

Colleges that have effective internal communication will find the implementation of innovation less disruptive because employees will have time to understand the proposal and its intended outcomes. Surprises are never suffered well by employees, particularly if internal relationships are already strained. Students must also be considered part of this communication plan.

I have also learned that which any good attorney knows. If you have a weakness in your rationale or argument, it should be presented upfront and owned. Otherwise, the opposing counsel will reveal it later, and most assuredly to their advantage. Similarly, if all the facts surrounding the proposed innovation are not revealed early, particularly the weaker points, some disgruntled employee will focus attention on the apparently concealed risk, rather than the potential rewards of the change. In planning for more significant or controversial disruptive innovations, many successful colleges have used open letters to employees, convocations, departmental meetings, one-on-one communications, and newsletters to communicate key messages.

In addition to a solid internal communications strategy, the president must also develop an external communications plan, especially since community colleges are a part of the community, and the public generally considers itself to be the owner of the college. When they occur, pubic attacks on projects come from detractors who may admit to knowing little to nothing about the project, nor any of the details surrounding the effort, but still maintain that the project is not right for the college.

Bloggers are becoming a particularly strong source of criticism. One of the best strategies to help in the promotion of innovation and change is to engage leaders from business partners who embrace the importance of innovation. They may serve as your chief supporters for innovative work. Bringing the public along in the discussion is important. Community forums and institutional publications are useful, as are public meetings of advisory committees, trustees, foundation boards, and others.

Community college change and innovation must be understood in our communities as a strategic weapon in the battle not only for relevancy, but also for the economic health of the community. By taking responsibility for a well-prepared, preemptive, and external communications plan that is transparent, logical, inclusive of early supporters, and distributed through multiple conduits, the college may be able to temper the assaults on the innovation.

On a few occasions, principally due to the public nature of most of the nation's community colleges, broad planning and open discussion on a change initiative plan may not be possible. For example, consider a college looking to acquire property that would advance its competitive advantage through strategic location, capacity, or the potential for new development. Negotiations, should they become public, could introduce new competitors, drive up the price, or give an early alert to rival institutions that may block or delay the sale.

In such cases, full community disclosure may not be beneficial. That said, even this type of decision should involve the board, key instructional leaders, a few trusted advisors in the community, and appropriate counsel from bankers, lawyers, and other potential partners. These opportunities are likely few and far between. In all cases though, as soon as possible after the transaction concludes, the president should inform the college and the community about the project with as many details as is practical.

As a more pragmatic example, in 2008, Michigan community college presidents and trustees decided to seek legislative authorization to award baccalaureate degrees in a number of career areas to better serve local students, similar to community colleges in over twenty other states. The Michigan leaders knew they were sailing into a perfect storm. In the distance there was one squall line comprised of the state's fifteen universities who saw this as "mission creep" for community colleges, and they wanted the initiative stopped.

A second squall line consisted of fifteen independent colleges and universities that, similarly, saw it as an intrusion into their already financially challenged existence, and finally, a third squall line contained a handful of private, for-profit, baccalaureate-granting colleges that did not want further competition in the marketplace.

Fully aware of the high seas ahead and the associated risks, the Michigan community colleges sailed into the storm, keenly focused upon the best interests of their students, many of whom were time-bound, place-bound, and financially challenged. The Michigan Community College Association (MCCA), as part of its planning and communication strategy, asked the state's Department of Labor and Economic Growth (DLEG) for an independent study of the need for additional baccalaureate degree holders in the state. DLEG worked with the legislature to draft a formal request to conduct the study.

The resulting report yielded data about the many benefits that community college baccalaureate-granting capacity would accrue for the state, its workforce, and its students. The data were shared with the legislature and the governor's office. Locally, community college presidents worked with their boards and institutional leaders to communicate to their employees and communities the intentions of the effort. Presidents also coordinated plans with their regional accrediting body. A number of legislative hearings were conducted in both House and Senate committee rooms in Lansing. Universities, independent colleges, and for-profit colleges, were given the opportunity to speak to the issue. Lobbying was fierce and intense for all sides.

At MCCA meetings, presidents and trustees evaluated the changing political landscape and the strategies of opponents. They created solid counter-communications. Key leaders in the Michigan House and the Senate were asked to drive support through their respective chambers. Four years later, in 2012, Michigan community colleges were granted authorization to award baccalaureate degrees in four vocational areas: cement technology, maritime technology, energy production technology, and culinary arts. A bachelor degree in nursing was initially included in the list, but it was removed in the final hours of negotiations.

The key points to note from this example are threefold. First, once an initiative is launched, the communications machinery must be dynamic, adaptive, and vigilant. Leadership needs to be on guard against the opposition's strategic presentation of information, which can infuse doubt in the minds of decision makers. In the worst cases, and disappointingly, the opposition may actually present facts that are patently false. Remaining proactive, flexible, and ready to respond at a moment's notice to the changing landscape is essential.

The second point is best explained by Simon Sinek, author of *Start with Why: How Great Leaders Inspire Everyone to Take Action.* In the book, Sinek asks about the purpose, cause, or belief that inspires us to do what we do. Sinek notes that the "why" is often overlooked in favor of the "what" or the "how" of an idea or initiative, but it is the "why" that calls people to take action.[28]

This "why" was the core message of the MCCA member presidents and Michigan community college trustees. By offering selected baccalaureate degrees, Michigan's community colleges provide students an opportunity to acquire specific knowledge and skills close to home, and, by extension, these baccalaureate degree holders help to advance the state's workforce and economy. Ultimately, it was the "why" message that won over the legislature and the governor.

The third point is of critical importance to planning and strategy. We had done our homework and built into our plan targeted goals, established timelines, relevant data, and a multilevel communications strategy not only to build support, but to educate as well.

Still, even with a plan, we were constantly adapting, responding with counter-communications, counter-testimonies, and aggressive legislative vote gathering. While we did not receive all the program approvals sought, such is the nature of the political process. At the time of this publication, requests for additional baccalaureate-level career program authorizations have been introduced into legislature and are being actively pursued.

One final caution is that institutional leaders must avoid the temptation to over-promise outcomes in an attempt to win support for the undertaking. The president and his or her team must be realistic about likely problem areas, avoid personal ego involvement, and pay close attention to others' knowledge and intentions, incorporating suggestions where advisable to do so. Credibility can be easily lost if a president is not forthright in his or her assessment of likely outcomes. In the case of the MCCA, retention of credibility was vital because, as previously noted, we are now seeking additional authorizations, to say nothing of future legislative support.

NOTES

1. Clayton M. Christensen et al., "Disrupting College: How Disruptive Innovation Can Deliver Quality and Affordability to Postsecondary Education." Washington, DC: Center for America Progress, (2011). Accessed January 3, 2014. https://www.americanprogress.org/issues/labor/report/2011/02/08/9034/disrupting-college/.

2. David B. Yoffie and Michael A. Cusumano, *Strategy Rules: Five Timeless Lessons from Bill Gates, Andy Grove, and Steve Jobs* (New York: HaperCollins Publishers, 2015), 93.

3. Ibid., 52.

4. Farhad Manjoo, "Uber's Business Model Could Change Your Work." *The New York Times*, Personal Tech Section, New York Edition, January 29, 2015, B1.

5. Collaborative Consumption: Sharing Reinvented through Technology, "Pioneer Interview with Gerard Kiely of MentorPitch." Accessed on May 25, 2015. http://www.collaborativeconsumption.com/2015/04/30/pioneer-interview-with-gerard-kiely-of-mentorpitch/.

6. Tamar Lewin, "Web-Era Trade Schools, Feeding a Need for Code." *The New York Times*, Education Section, New York Edition. October 14, 2014, A1. Accessed May 25, 2015. http://www.nytimes.com/2014/10/14/us/web-era-trade-schools-feeding-a-need-for-code.html?ref=education&_r=0.

7. Jeffrey R. Young, "Wearable Teaching? College to Experiment with Apple Watch as Learning Tool." *Chronicle of Higher Education*, April 27, 2015. Accessed on May 25, 2015. http://chronicle.com/blogs/wiredcampus/wearable-teaching-college-to-experiment-with-apple-watch-as-learning-tool/56459.

8. Laura G. Knapp, Janice E. Kelly-Reid, and Scott A. Ginder, *Postsecondary Institutions and Price of Attendance in 2011-12, Degrees and Other Awards Conferred: 2010-11, and 12-Month Enrollment: 2010-11: First Look (Provisional Data)*, NCES 2012-289reve (Washington, DC: U.S. Department of Education, National Center for Education Statistics, 2012), in Josh S. Wyner, *What Excellent Community Colleges Do: Preparing All Students for Success* (Cambridge, MA: Harvard Education Press, 2014), 120.

9. Josh S. Wyner, *What Excellent Community Colleges Do: Preparing All Students for Success*, 120.

10. Kenneth A. Ender, personal communication. February 8, 2015.

11. *Community College Daily*, "Harper Launches Scholarship to Cover Two Years." March 30, 2015. Accessed on May 25, 2015. http://ccdaily.com/Pages/Campus-Issues/Harper-launches-scholarship-to-cover-two-years.aspx.

12. Kelsey Sheehy, "Dorms Help Give 2-year Colleges a 4-Year Feel: At Some Community Colleges, Students Can Still Get a Traditional College Experience." *U.S. News & World Report*. Accessed June 13, 2015. http://www.usnews.com/education/community-colleges/articles/2015/02/09/dorms-help-give-2-year-colleges-a-4-year-feel.

13. Peter Drucker, *Managing in Turbulent Times*. New York: Routledge, Taylor & Francis, 1980, 227.

14. John P. Kotter, *Leading Change* (Boston, MA: Harvard Business School Press, 2012), 131.

15. Ibid., 22–24.

16. Mike Doyle, Tim Claydon, and Dave Buchanan, "Mixed Results, Lousy Process: the Management Experience of Organizational Change." *British Journal of Management*, 11:2000, S72.

17. Yoffie and Cusumano, *Strategy Rules: Five Timeless Lessons from Bill Gates, Andy Grove, and Steve Jobs*.

18. Richard Rhodes, personal communication, February 27, 2015.

19. Christine Sobek, personal communication, November 25, 2014.

20. David Duncan, "Driving Front Line Innovation in Health Care." *Harvard Business Review* (April 15, 2013). Accessed on May 8, 2015. https://hbr.org/2013/04/driving-front-line-innovation.

21. Henry Stancu, "SickKids, Project Horizon: Hospital's Plan for the Future." *The Toronto Star*. Published May 6, 2015. Accessed June 13, 2015. http://www.thestar.com/life/sick_kids/2015/05/06/sickkids-project-horizon-hospitals-plan-for-the-future.html.

22. Chris Bustamante, personal communication, November 25, 2014.

23. Scott Anthony, David Duncan, and Pontus Siren, "Building an Innovation Engine in 90 Days." *Harvard Business Review* 92, 12 (2014): 61–68.

24. Ibid., 61–68.

25. Bergen Community College, "Center for Innovation and Learning." Accessed November 23, 2014. http://www.bergen.edu/faculty-staff/center-for-innovation-in-teaching-and-learning/our-staff.

26. Adam Lashinsky, *Inside Apple: How America's Most Admired and Secretive Company Really Works* (London: John Murray Publishers, 2012).

27. Mick Starcevich, Personal Communication, June 3, 2014.

28. Simon Sinek, *Start with Why: How Great Leaders Inspire Everyone to Take Action* (London: Penguin Books, 2009).

SIX

Innovation Implementation, Evaluation, and Efficacy

"Innovation distinguishes between a leader and a follower."
—Steve Jobs

Incrementalism is not transformation. Maintaining a course of modest improvements in piecemeal fashion will never position your college for long-term success. Without a robust, comprehensive, and implemented strategy of change and innovation, your institution will be destined to slog from one minimalist action to another.

The purpose of this book is to encourage organizational leaders to "see the whole chessboard," and in so doing, bring leaders, their employees, and institutions to a point of embracing change and innovation as standard operational practices in the new economy. Our challenge is to make meaningful, frame-breaking, consequential advancements in our industry. This happens through the steadfast pursuit of a plan for change and innovation at your college, and ultimately the execution of the particular change initiative or project.

As a leader, it is you who ultimately will execute the change and innovation strategy you have created, monitor its progress, keep it on a steady course to its terminus, and consider the experience along the journey, using the knowledge gained to inform the next initiative.

THE SCIENCE OF IMPLEMENTING AND ADVANCING CHANGE

When examining strategy for implementing change, many researchers emerge with a formula. For example, through his research of multiple organizations, Gleicher divined a technical approach that recognizes not

121

only the unique features of change, but also the critical elements to be addressed for its successful advancement:

1. There must be organizational dissatisfaction with current practices, operations, or the way things work generally;
2. The vision of the institutional transformation must be well articulated; and
3. The implementation plan must be well defined and broadly communicated.

Without these three requirements being met, it is highly probable, according to Gleicher, that the initiative will not succeed.

The formula for change involves three variables and can be expressed as a mathematical equation. The variables help researchers to determine the level of meaning ascribed by employees to the proposed changes, their relative level of resistance, and finally, whether or not the resistance can be overcome. Often referred to as Gleicher's formula, it is expressed as $D \times V \times F > R = \Delta$.

D: Dissatisfaction levels among employees with the current situation.

V: Vision of the goal, what can be done, and implication for employees.

F: First steps of the plan to be undertaken toward realizing the vision.

R: Resistance levels among employees to change.

Δ: Probability of success with the change or innovation intended.[1]

Through the use of this formulaic tool, it is suggested that organizational leaders can better implement and manage change and innovation. The methodology suggests that innovation and change are only possible when D, V, and F are greater than the resistance to change. If any of these variables is considered low, the likelihood of persisting to any level of success is also quite low. Consider each of the variables more fully below:

D: Dissatisfaction with the Current Situation

When employees are satisfied with the current state of the organization and their role within it, they have little or no incentive to change that state. Therefore, to create the motivation for employees to change, the administration must present information that outlines why the current situation is problematic, how it might negatively affect them in the future, and how the new opportunity could benefit them.

Essentially, leaders must draw employees toward a new goal or a new way of doing things. Furthermore, leaders must establish a sense of urgency regarding the need for the change, and this must emanate from a rationale that employees believe to be valid and reasonable.

V: Vision of the Possibilities

A clear vision of the future, a plan for implementation, and an understanding of how it will affect employees personally are central to employees' willingness to undertake the goal. The role of the community college leader is to provide a single, complete, and compelling picture of the desired end state.

There must be a tangible understanding of plan implementation, timelines, potential challenges, and what goal achievement looks like. Why? Because any confusion about the singular view of the future could cause employees to suspect double-speak, or to lose motivation to keep moving the plan forward.

As noted previously, it is important that leaders avoid ambiguity when they discuss the future. The clearer the leader can be with employees about the plan or a particular initiative, the more likely the employees will be drawn to it and enthusiastic about working toward its realization.

F: First Steps Toward Change

This variable involves the strategy that will be used to achieve the goals of the plan. Employees want to understand not only the vision, but also see the roadway to get there. They want to understand the plan in some detail: the timelines, intended obligations for the organization and themselves, resource requirements, and workload implications. The degree of detail sought by each employee will vary based upon his or her level of interest, or his or her level of trust in the administration. A perceived low level of risk of failure, coupled with a high potential of success, will help to secure their involvement.

Leadership must provide the edification necessary, and present it at a level that is able to be widely understood, to assure employees that the vision is reasonable and that a solid action plan has been developed for goal attainment.[2] It is vital to avoid disconnects between plan implementation efforts, and the staff who will be engaged in the process.

THE POWER OF INFORMATION, KNOWLEDGE, AND EXPERIENCE

Gleicher's formula creates a unique vantage point from which the challenges of advancing innovation and change can be examined. One related point to consider, suggests Anne Kress, president of Monroe Community College in New York, is perspective. In her view, one of the basic challenges for leaders in advancing innovation is remaining cognizant of the fact that leaders typically have information, and thus context, from which others are insulated.

Presidents are besieged by information that carries a strong and steady mandate for change, from federal and state directives, publications and reports, conference sessions, trustees, and the community. According to President Kress, "We assume everyone knows this information, but the fact of the matter is that others are not part of these conversations. To others, it can look like we are interested in change for change's sake. We need to give them what they need to know, presented at a level that is understandable, so that they have the opportunity to arrive at the same conclusions we have. That's on us."[3]

One strategy for closing this information gap is investing heavily in communications and professional development opportunities so that others in the organization receive relevant and timely information. Convocations and all-employee meetings are best, though videos and distributed communications can be helpful, too. More powerful still is the utilization of cross-functional teams of administration, faculty, and staff who attend training programs and conferences together. This is not only an effective strategy for obtaining information, but it can also help to break down barriers and build relationships.

As an example of disconnect between plan and staff at an institutional level, President Kress told me about her experience with declining enrollment following the post–Great Recession economic recovery. She met with faculty department chairs (those elected by the faculty with no administrative appointment) at their request. They expressed concern about their classes being cut from the schedule, and wanted to know why.

President Kress immediately recognized the knowledge gap between her reactionary plan and the faculty's knowledge base. The enrollment data that she reviewed regularly, which clearly pointed to the need for schedule recalibration, wasn't available in a digestible format to faculty chairs, so it had no bearing on their analysis or perception.

She noted that they did not have time to plow through the raw data and arrive at the same conclusions that she had. She said, "I resolved to help them get access to the information they needed. So, I asked them, 'What are the top three things you want to know?' and I now get this information to them routinely. We have to help them."[4] President Kress's advice is an important touchstone for all community college leaders, to remind us to ensure that our message is understood, and in the manner intended.

Keely Wilson and Yves Doz, global innovation authors, have developed ten helpful guidelines for introducing and managing innovation, following a study of 186 companies representing seventeen industrial sectors across nineteen countries. They describe the value of fully defining the innovation being sought. The authors note that "everything must be defined up front: the product or service architecture, the functionality . . . process flows, timelines, and knowledge requirements need to be thoroughly understood so that everyone working on the project has the same understanding of the goals and their individual contributions to them."[5]

The notion to move forward is tempting. However, the authors draw a strong positive correlation between project success and the amount of time spent defining goals and the structure of the project to employees. As an example, they cite Essilor, a manufacturer of corrective lenses that sought to leapfrog the industry with the creation of a new, more effective and innovative type of photochromic lenses (optical lenses that are clear, but can darken on exposure to specific types of light, particularly ultraviolet radiation).

Even though the company believed that it didn't have much time to bring the new innovation to market because of the aggressive competition in the industry, the company still dedicated nine months working with employees to painstakingly define the idea, product specifications, and action steps for taking the product to market. In so doing, the company was successful in bringing their new product enhancement to market before others, they did so effectively, and equally important, they also built trust with employees.

This type of action underscores the importance of prework before a plan is launched. This dedication not only to process, but also to people, is particularly important with employees of different cultures and nationalities, as Essilor understood. Employee diversity, whether geographic, ethnic, or demographic, requires special attention, especially when the work is global. Leaders must use care in appreciating how diverse populations perceive communications. The avoidance of a one-size-fits-all communication strategy, style, and mediatype is respectful to others, enhancing employee and administration relationships, it also seeks to ensure an understanding among employees, which is essential to effective implementation.

INITIATIVE VALIDATION

How does your organization ensure that its elected initiative is the "right" one, and not an incorrect or narrow interpretation of environmental data? How do you ensure that the selected project has not been unduly influenced by cultural bias, personal interest, or politics? It is prudent to implement a system of validation for the proposed innovation, especially given the limited resources of most community colleges and the potential for project failure and negative political fallout.

The verification of an innovation's significance as a goal may be accomplished through questioning. Paul Shoemaker, research director of the Mack Institute for Innovation Management at the Wharton School of the University of Pennsylvania, and Steven Krupp, president of Decision Strategies International (DSI), argue that most successful innovation thinkers and achievers regularly frame questions for themselves and others during the early consideration and leadership of an initiative.

The authors question whether, through the intended innovation, the right problem has been identified. As an example of the benefit of questioning, they cite IBM, which had the opportunity to acquire a new reprographic photo process from Xerox in the 1960s. IBM was focused on remaining a market leader by making faster, cheaper, and more reliable copiers, with an emphasis on understanding how many more copies, from originals the average person would need in a given year (note: The available technology of the day only provided copies from the original document).

Both companies attempted to develop a calculus for the number, but IBM's perspective limited the framing of the right question (i.e., copies from original documents). This led to a lost opportunity for IBM. Had IBM queried how the new Xerox technology might change the way people make copies, meaning copies from copies, together with the total number of copies from copies the average person might need, the outcome might have been different. Instead, IBM lost out on owning the technology that we all know and appreciate today.[6]

Still, inquiry alone is no panacea for selection of the right innovation to pursue. Indeed, the nature of the question, or the manner in which questioning is pursued, can create its own set of biases, thereby negating the purpose it sought to serve. The authors note, "The questions leaders pose sometimes get in the way of solving the right problem or seeing more innovative solutions. They are often too narrow, overly protective of the current business, or assume that the old habits, business models and regulations will remain largely intact."[7] Therefore, it seems prudent to be vigilant regarding our thoughts, biases, and inquiries when we consider possible scenarios and targets for innovative pursuits. The way we frame questions can undermine our success.

Effective questions, especially those aimed at encouraging dialogue and creative thinking, are open-ended. For example, in considering information technology on campus we might ask our technical staff, "In what ways can we use Cloud-based technologies and environments to benefit our students?" After a thought-provoking question, we must then listen without judgment, asking for clarification from them only as needed. We must observe their emotions, forcefulness, use of words, and their conclusions, all without rushing to dispel their thoughts in favor of our own preformed opinions.

If we can find the space and discipline to support creative and honest questioning, there is much to be learned, especially since the process provides a forum to uncover ideas that we might never have considered. Through consistently modeling purposeful questioning and active listening, we may begin to build a mindful and innovative organizational culture.

The concept of "mindfulness" has been around for decades, though it was only recently popularized by Ellen Langer, professor of psychology at Harvard University, who suggests that mindfulness can be defined as the simple act of actively noticing things.[8] After forty years of research, Langer argues, "When you [notice new things], it puts you in the present. It makes you more sensitive to context and perspective. It's the essence of engagement."[9]

To illustrate the link between mindfulness and innovation, Langer conducted a study in which she asked participants to come up with new uses for products that had failed. She prepared the first study group for *mindlessness* (the action of following routine and rules) by telling them how the product (a failed 3M glue) had fallen short of its intended use, but resulted in Post-It notes. She then prepared the second study group for *mindfulness* (actively noticing new things) by describing the product's characteristics: a substance that adheres for only a short time. As we might expect, the most creative ideas for new uses came from the second group.[10]

For community college leaders, the reframing of institutional and environmental issues may provide solutions that we might have overlooked initially. According to Langer, a great place to start in creating a more mindful organization is to be vigilant in avoiding mindlessness by developing a comfort with uncertainty and openness to new ideas. She notes, "You can be mindless only if two conditions are met: You found the very best way of doing things, and nothing changes."[11] In an environment filled with constant change, where we cannot possibly know everything, this shouldn't be the case. We just need to embrace mindfulness.

I find Langer's discussion about attentiveness as part of mindfulness to be insightful and useful for community college leaders in their selection and validation of change initiatives. Moving beyond autopilot settings can free us from the status quo and its perpetuation. Heightening our attention to the things around us, particularly with an eye and mind toward the future, is how we will foster greater potential for innovation and long-term success.

Decision making and risk taking contribute to a full plate of responsibilities for the community college leader, and mindfulness can help take some of the pressure off. Research has demonstrated that mindfulness yields positive outcomes in the people who practice it, including better health, happiness, and increased competence. Mindfulness can give new meaning to our experiences, and through the use of creativity, ideas, and words, meaning is amplified. Mindfulness also underscores that as institutional leaders we do not need to control everything ourselves.

Langer proposes that we embrace the fact that leaders don't know what is coming next, while remaining confident that our colleges can deal with whatever happens. Langer says, "I tell leaders they should make 'not knowing' OK. . . . Get people to ask, 'Why? What are the benefits of doing it this way versus another way?' When you do that, you're all better able to see and take advantage of opportunities."

As leaders we should not make the unknown bigger than it has to be. Mindfully reframing the pursuit of the future as an enjoyable practice for our organization can improve the experience for all involved. Still, this approach needs to be balanced against reality and practical considerations. As Langer puts it, "When faced with complex issues and conflicting information, it is easy to fool yourself: If you torture the data hard enough, it will confess to almost anything!"[12]

CONNECTING INNOVATION TO PLAN DEPLOYMENT

The way innovation systems, strategy, and deployment work varies by organization, particularly as it relates to the size of the organization. Tony Davila, Marc Epstein, and Robert Shelton note that in smaller organizations innovation occurs almost naturally as part of the work of the company, particularly in entrepreneurial and small businesses.

> For example, a single inventor or group of collaborators may launch a company with one robust idea. But as organizations expand, innovation does not happen anymore as a natural occurrence—the right people may not interact, the information may not flow to the right places, and the motivation to take risks may diminish. Organizations as large as General Electric or Proctor & Gamble may develop silos—compartmentalized departments that barely communicate with each other, much less strive to innovate. This is why larger organizations need systems to manage innovation.[13]

Gary Pisano, business administration professor and member of the U.S. Competitiveness Project at Harvard Business School, states that in order to effectively launch an innovation strategy, there should be

> a clear understanding and articulation of specific objectives related to helping the company achieve sustainable competitive advantage. This requires going beyond all-too-common generalities, such as "We must innovate to grow," or "We need to innovate to stay ahead of competitors." Those are not strategies. They provide no sense of the types of innovation that might matter (and those that won't). Rather, a robust innovation strategy should answer the following questions: How will this innovation create value for potential customers? How will the company capture a share of the value its innovations create? What types of innovations will allow the company to create and capture value and what resources should each type receive?[14]

Such observations, though not new to the research covered thus far, do drive the organization's leadership to the pathway by which the innovation will be realized. What remains now in the implementation process is to identify the resources necessary to undertake it.

RESOURCING THE PLAN

Beyond the development of plans and strategies is the practicality of capitalizing upon the new culture and bringing forward actual initiatives and resourcing them. Jeff Marsee, former CFO and CAO of numerous colleges, and currently CEO of Marsee and Associates, an independent management consulting firm, suggests engaging "change missionaries." These are "committed individuals who are willing to step away from the status quo . . . driven by a belief that their cause is correct and the outcome will better serve the organization. These individuals may not have the drive to be in the spotlight typically exhibited by change agents. However, when it comes to providing the muscle to get the work done, this group of core supporters makes the difference." [15]

He also encourages collaboration with "change agents." He characterizes these employees as "individuals who believe they must initiate action to improve organizational effectiveness. They thrive in an environment where change is the norm." [16] It is both groups, when combined with the college's leadership, who are responsible for the fourth batten: Innovation Execution and Evaluation.

If you are considering structural change as part of the implementation process, decision makers need to address administrative hierarchy. When new organizational systems are implemented, it is the middle managers who have the most to lose. They are caught between accountability to senior leaders and responsibility for addressing inertia and resistance among faculty and staff.

Middle managers are the worker bees that top leaders must rely upon for the execution of innovation. College deans and directors, by their words and actions, determine the success or failure of the venture. This reality cannot be lost on the college president and must become part of his or her strategy.

Staffing is not the only resource consideration necessary for success. Other points to consider include the following:

- How will our organization support an ongoing culture of innovation?
- Where does responsibility for innovation exist in a community college?
- To whom does it report?
- Who manages communication — the good and the bad?
- What are the specific points of accountability regarding our effectiveness?

Clear and formal organizational structures, as well as ongoing reporting and accountability, are indispensable.

Final considerations include funding and the sustainability thereof. Marsee says, "It is essential that organizations create or set aside dedicated funds to invest in the development and implementation of innovation. In a perennially resource-constrained environment, where and how an organization spends scarce resources demonstrates its commitment to shifting the culture."[17]

This commitment can be part of an ongoing budgeting process, a specific project-oriented allocation, an application of external resources, or some combination of the three. Regardless, sustainability is the key. Construction projects cannot begin until sufficient resources and commitment are secured to ensure completion, and so should be the case with innovation, regardless of the size of the effort.

At Cambridge College in Massachusetts, for example, "President Deborah Jackson offers financial incentives to her faculty teams to encourage the design of new models for business, educational, and organizational change at the college. Winning prototype designs are pitched to the executive team and the best of the bunch are provided $1,500 to further develop their prototypes to improve the college's offerings. 'To create a culture of innovation, it does require vision, skills, resources, and a plan,' says Jackson, 'but I think you also incentivize people to act. By funding our prototype cycles, our faculty know we are serious about prototyping tomorrow.'"[18] For particular projects, however, more substantial quantities of funding may be required.

Given that community colleges are largely under-resourced, we must give careful consideration to which initiatives to fund, and how much to invest. This is advisable because the state funds many community colleges receive tend to be discretionary. Likewise, tuition derived from enrollment levels is dynamic. And for some community colleges, local property taxes can also be a variable source of revenue. Therefore, it is prudent for administrators to employ a level of conservatism in deploying the general fund. Unless the college has a skilled and successful grant writer, a well-heeled foundation, or an angel donor, there may not be many financial resource options. For most community colleges, if a new proposal is to be realized, it will require the reallocation of existing funds.

Sometimes, those decisions come down to closing, or "cannibalizing," an existing effort, as was often the case for Steve Jobs. David Yoffie and Michael Cusumano researched the leadership styles of Steve Jobs, Andy Grove, and Bill Gates and found some rather interesting parallels. For example, they concluded that advancing innovation sometimes requires the leader to deconstruct some aspect of current operations for the sake of releasing needed funds, which they call "cannibalization."

They further conclude that "[it] can mean trading known success for an unknown future: trading highly profitable sales for unknown margins; and even trading dollars for dimes. . . . Making problems even worse, cannibalization creates winners and losers within an organization."[19]

As a practical example, the authors note that despite the strong sales volume for the Apple iPod Mini in 2005, Steve Jobs, who was focused on continued development of the Apple Nano, gave the order to kill further production of the iPod Mini. He did so before the company had completely developed and tested the Nano, let alone launched it. Of course the bet paid off for Jobs and Apple with even higher sales volume once the Nano came to market.

Some days, as community college leaders, the stakes in decision making about institutional budgets and innovation funding can feel almost as onerous as Jobs' decision making at Apple, Inc. For Jobs, and I believe for community colleges, marketplace urgency and advancing competition suggest that simply waiting for others to take the lead, or surrendering to the status quo, are no longer options. Jobs was a visionary who was vigilant in tracking the changing technological environment and his customers, and who did what he believed needed to be done to remain the best in the industry.

VIGILANCE

For years, I've watched my father-in-law on our sailboat. He is a physician by training and a sailor of his own making. I have noticed his disciplined and constant attention to the sails when we put to sea. At times I have asked him, "What do you see?" More often than not he will describe the curve of the sail, and explain that he is reading the telltales.

The behavior of the telltales can instruct a sailor to further trim (adjust) the sail for better performance. My father-in-law is constantly experimenting with sails and lines, just to see what will happen. I can nearly hear him thinking, "If I take this action on the sail, will it make things better or worse?"

He observes action and reaction, makes mental notes, and files them away for when they may become relevant. Even when he looks across the water, he does not gaze like you or I might, taking in the grand view. Rather, he looks intently. When I ask him what he sees then, he tells me that he is "reading the water" for variation, changes in wind conditions, and water patterns, all in order to best prepare or position the boat and the sails.

In sailing, I used to be content, for the most part, to have the boat moving merrily forward on a great sunny day. I have read the manuals, but it took time before I noticed what he noticed. I had not trained myself to be a keen observer, vigilant to what was happening around me. I had not connected observations (emergent situations) with corresponding specific actions (solutions). My father-in-law was not content with the craft's forward movement. He is a consummate student of sailing.

A similar vigilance is key for college leaders. Monitoring the telltales of the college, so to speak, making course corrections, and watching for clues will provide some degree of anticipation of what is to come. It's important to be ready for an innovation or change. When I consider emulating my father-in-law's sailing characteristics in my own field, I consider what attributes community college leaders must embody for navigation, experimentation, investment, and operational adjustment. Curiosity? Focus? Confidence?

BUSINESS MODELS MUST MATCH MISSION

Unlike businesses, community colleges don't have the ability to issue debt, sell stock options, or launch an initial public offering (IPO) to generate more income. Therefore, we must think differently—innovatively. Community colleges have been around for more than one hundred years, yet our operating and business models are virtually the same as when the colleges were created.

How is this conceivable when the demands and expectations are fundamentally different? Our institutions were originally designed for *student access*, not *student success*. Research shows that our community college progenitors sought to position a community college within a fifty-mile radius of every American.

Today, while access continues to be a priority for community colleges, it is not the only focus, or even the primary focus. Still, we continue to apply an access-based business model to a now success-focused industry instead of changing to a success-based business model. For me, this realization comes at a time when it seems that the public is increasingly disinclined to view a community college education, if not all of higher education, as a public good, and therefore, disinclined to support it at optimum levels. Our attempts at prioritizing and moving toward student success and completion tend to be limited in scope, with efforts largely limited by resource availability.

An example includes community college "boutique" programs that are models of successful practice. Achievement and student demographic-based programs funded by TRIO, Title III and other such initiatives demonstrate how intensive, low teacher/mentor-to-student ratios, say 1:15–20, can significantly improve student success.

In 2008 Jackson College developed an internal initiative called Men of Merit, which serves approximately thirty to fifty African-American males annually. Student performance data show that their persistence levels exceed that of all African-American males on campus, as well as the general student population, at over 90 percent from semester to semester. Their academic performance rates also exceed that of all African-American males at the college.

As part of the entry requirement into the program, Men of Merit conducts a personal life assessment for each student, to better understand his unique situation. Program Director Lee Hampton and his staff conduct multiple group meetings over the course of the academic year wherein students are actively engaged, and attendance is required. Activities include discussing their educational and life experiences, interacting with leaders of color who discuss their pathway to success, and mentoring other students of color.

These men are engaged in the life of the college and the community, committing hundreds of service hours to various organizations. Students are required to attend classes and study sessions, and their participation is monitored. In fact, the program is replete with accountability, not only from Hampton, but from peer students as well. As you might imagine, given the intensity and coordination of such a program, it is quite expensive.

With three full-time, dedicated staff to provide extensive programming and support, and other operational costs, taking the program to scale, that is, deploying the program across the entire student population, is infeasible. This is the unfortunate, yet recurring, challenge with student success-focused boutique programs. For the most part, unless other significant and sustainable revenue streams become available, these programs remain at a small scale.

To be sure, colleges do what they can to reallocate funds, seeking grants and investing more in such programs whenever possible. However, the lesson from this and other boutique programs is that the success of proven innovative programs is limited if a new business model is not part of the equation.

Such a model requires a serious discussion about the cost of providing a high-quality education, which must take into consideration the academic readiness of incoming students and desired outcomes. There must also be a recognition that the profile of the community college student — preparedness, demographic, motivation, and generational status — is unlike the profile of university students.

Therefore, in order to make significant gains in student success and completion, there must be a significantly improved funding stream to support it. Until federal and state governments should accept their responsibility to help provide for a learned populous, community colleges will continue to struggle with providing high-quality education with high-level outcomes on the cheap.

Interestingly, public commentary suggests that higher education is a private good; therefore, as the logic goes, postsecondary consumers of higher education should pay for it. One might conclude that the reduction in support nationally, combined with increasing accountability, is a nod to this belief. Sadly, the only remaining vehicle, beyond gifts and time-limited grants, involves raising tuition to a level that will support student success on a larger scale.

Raising tuition beyond the typical CPI, or the $1–2 per credit hour per year, is a radical idea, to say the least, regardless of how significant the proposed innovation. However, the current model is not working. Nationally, roughly 31 percent of community college students complete an associate degree and advance to earn a bachelor degree. Only 21 percent ever complete an associate degree.[20]

The success data of students enrolled in community college developmental education programs are likewise troubling. The majority of students entering community colleges are not ready for collegiate prime time in reading, writing, or mathematics. More often than not, it will be math that snares the entering student.

Interestingly, some 30 percent of the remedial-placed students don't even show up for their first class. Only 40 percent of developmental education students finish their developmental courses, fewer still if they need help in all three subject areas.[21] Our students do not arrive with the intention of failing or dropping out. At some point, then, this becomes an ethical question, if not a moral dilemma. Do we continue to take tuition dollars from students, knowing that the vast majority will fail, some without earning a single credit hour? Or do we bring the intensive staffing resources to bear in order to increase the likelihood of student success?

Implementing a client-based design wherein college staff are specifically assigned to a cohort of students, making multiple contacts over the course of a semester, tracking their progress, and encouraging them along the way, is long overdue. However, this model requires staff, and a lot of them.

Similarly, faculty need manageable class sizes to enable them to assess whether students are making progress, to work with those needing extra help, and to refer them for additional support as needed. Furthermore, adjunct faculty need to be adequately trained to provide support to students, and even to make students aware of the multiple college resources available to them. The point here is not to criticize the good work of community colleges, but rather to suggest that the majority of community college students need close-in support and instruction.

Community colleges need more personnel to achieve the objective of improved student completion. Plainly, the current community college business and operational models are perfectly designed to give us precisely the results we are getting. We can't have it both ways—low tuition and high student completion—without the intensive support of personnel. Our boutique programs tell us this.

Part of the work of innovation is for leaders to ensure that the initiative or objective has the resources necessary to be successful. Another part of innovative leadership is to reevaluate existing systems and business models, for example, reconsideration of the revenue model. Rather than a traditional, tuition-based model, perhaps a subscription-based revenue model wherein students are incentivized to take any number of courses for a fixed period of time, for a flat rate, would drive completion. Or perhaps a completion-based model, with a 10 percent cash-back guarantee, might incentivize the success agenda. There are myriad innovative designs to consider.

Saul Kaplan notes that product reengineering, benchmarking, continuous quality improvement practices, and the related tweaking that have been effective through the end of an industrial era, are no longer sufficient. His challenge is to develop new markets built around new practices, products, services, technologies, and business models. This approach can be summarized in a word: Transformative. Kaplan puts it this way:

> Leaders could get away with blindly focusing on a single business model in the twentieth century, when business models rarely changed. Most industrial era leaders never had to change their business model. One model worked throughout their entire careers. They could focus on improving their market position and competitiveness by making incremental improvements to the existing model. Disruptive threats were rare and could be safely ignored. Not so in the twenty-first century, when the half-life or longevity of a business model is decreasing. Business models just don't last as long as they used to. New players are rapidly emerging, enabled by disruptive technology, refusing to play by industrial-era rules.[22]

Simply, community college leaders need to develop organizational, operational, and budgetary tools and capabilities for success in this new frontier of higher education, in which higher education is becoming commoditized and college credits and degrees are fungible.

Jeff Immelt, CEO of General Electric, supports Kaplan's assertions and removes any doubt about the future of those who fail to adapt to the new economy. Speaking of the post–Great Recession era, Immelt says, "[I]t doesn't represent a cycle. It represents a reset. . . . It's an emotional, social, and economic reset . . . people who understand that will prosper. Those who don't will be left behind. There are going to be elements of the economy that will never be the same, ever."[23]

Higher education has largely held off entry into this "reset" space under the premise that higher education is different than business. It is widely held, particularly among faculty, that students are not our customers, and colleges are, in fact, the place where innovation, clarity of thought, debate, and dialogue can occur unfettered. However, higher education is out of time. The barbarians are at the gate, and they are an unhappy lot. Like Blockbuster, we have taken too long to react, and we now need to move faster to stay in the game.

As Kaplan observes, this issue faces leaders in all types of organizations. "Any organization that wants to be relevant, to deliver value at scale, and to sustain itself must clearly articulate and evolve its business model. And if an organization doesn't have a sustainable business model, its days are numbered."[24] As leaders, we might feel like the need to innovate is being forced upon us due to economics, competition, or necessity. Forced or not, organizational survival requires adaptation, innovation, or even the anticipation of essential market and operational changes. To be sure, there are many difficult decisions and areas to focus on for any innocation leader.

ADVANCING THE PLAN

When finally armed with a deeper understanding of disruptive innovation, sustaining innovation, change in general, and the powerful influence of existing culture, and in possession of needed resources, the community college president is prepared to advance an innovation plan. Central to this advancement, as stated previously, is a clear value proposition. If all requirements are satisfied, the institutional focus may shift to implementation.

One of the most vital characteristics of successful, innovative, plan-advancing presidents is their desire to improve upon the current situation. Competent leaders trust their gut, bring a lot of personal energy to the undertaking, and keep their eye firmly on the vision. Resilience is essential as well.

Presidents who are successful in advancing innovation are not damaged by the failure of a project. Rather, they view failure as part of the entrepreneurial process. They pick themselves up, evaluate what happened, learn from it, establish markers for avoidance strategies in the future, and move on.

In observing this resilience in other presidents, I notice that it seems to happen without committees, hand-wringing, or dragged-out discussions. The presidents just move on. At first blush, this behavior seems antithetical to higher education, where analysis paralysis is a common condition. However, the strongest presidents are appropriately measured and confident. In this way, they serve as a model for others in the pursuit of innovation.

INNOVATION PROJECT IMPLEMENTATION MANAGEMENT

Implementation of an innovative project requires ongoing management through its conclusion. Even then the work is not complete insofar as a post-hoc evaluation should be performed. Project management protocols will vary among organizations. However, Marsee suggests that regardless of design, management protocols must minimally include six assurances that guide the process:

1. Detailed key milestones and a projected completion date;
2. Awareness by implementation personnel of possible barriers, with alternative plans at the ready, and personnel assigned responsibility;
3. Project termination parameters that explain options should any barrier become intransigent;
4. Detailed communications protocols and project performance monitoring strategies;
5. Established processes in the event of unforeseen issues. The inevitability of these "unpredicted factors," as noted on the SAIL graphic, cannot be over-emphasized, nor over-detailed. The management team must be mindful of characteristically untimely arrival, and remain flexible in responding; and
6. Periodic progress review and described adjustment methods, as well as continuing commitment and support. [25]

Similarly, Jeffery Hiatt and Timothy Creasy encourage leaders to consider the unique aspects and dimensions of their organizations and to customize project management plans accordingly. They suggest that the plan should optimally be comprised of subplans or components including

1. Communications Plan: encompasses messages and medium that must be delivered to the project team members, based upon their individual roles;
2. Coaching Plan: designed to assist the employee's direct supervisor who supports and manages the employee through the change process;
3. Training Plan: as the name implies, seeks to build knowledge and skills regarding change;
4. Sponsor Road Map: recognizes the role of the leader and clarifies sponsor activities to help him or her carry out the management plan; and
5. Resistance Management Plan: provides guidance for working through opposition from employees as the project advances. [26]

Depending on the nature of the project and goal, progress monitoring could take as little as a few months, as in the case of moving a server-based office software suite to a cloud-based system, for example.

Conversely, the monitoring process for an initiative like college-wide cultural redefinition could require a protracted period of time—in some cases, even years. In the latter scenario, the organizational leader will need to be steadfast and persistent, and not lose focus or interest, because if he or she becomes distracted, so too will the organization. If the initiative is important enough to undertake, it is important enough to merit consistent attention until it is done.

As a pragmatic example, in 2009 at Monroe Community College, President Kress knew as a new leader to the institution that it would take considerable time to evaluate the culture of the college and determine where to make adjustments in the pursuit of vital goals. She needed a specific strategy.

To that end, she began working with the college's Special Committee on Administrative Affairs and the Faculty Senate to consider possible changes in the college's organizational structure, specifically those elements she perceived to be hindering progress.

President Kress quickly learned from the various groups that there was concern about the lack of clarity around individual job duties that had developed over time as job assignments changed but job descriptions did not change accordingly. In fact, the job descriptions were quite dated. The organizational structure was antiquated, with a tier-based advancement system that was inconsistent and difficult to understand.

President Kress began collaborating with union leaders, encouraging them to be part of the process and to help create buy-in. The president noted that "while we didn't get everything that we wanted, as long as you respect the process and commit to the time needed, you can eventually get what you need."[27]

Community colleges are often praised for their adaptability, flexibility, and responsiveness. Monroe Community College demonstrated these characteristics, for example, when area businesses requested modifications to existing programs to meet their needs. The college's faculty and staff responded by creating condensed certifications that students were able to complete in six months. This adaptation was implemented in only a few months.

According to President Kress, the changes ultimately resulted in programs that were more viable to industry, and students having jobs more quickly than otherwise would have occurred.[28] The challenge for leaders is to expedite the implementation of particular parts of processes where possible, but exercise restraint where needed, so as not to jeopardize the project—and to know the difference between the two.

Timing is only one component of management, and good management can temper unpredictable or less-than-ideal timing in the implementation of change. Regardless of the timeline required, though, failure to closely manage the implementation process, once designed, would be irresponsible. For it is the management of the process and the implementation of the systems designed that move innovation from an idea to a reality.

Indeed, Hiatt and Creasy define the implementation and management of change as the "application of processes and tools to manage the people side of change from a current state to a new future state so that the desired results of the change (and expected return on investment) are achieved."[29]

By this logic, it also makes sense to keep people at the front, middle, and the end of management planning, as well as the implementation process. Their continued involvement builds buy-in and ongoing commitment. Give them credit along the way whenever possible. Remember that alone, as leaders, we can do nothing. Change is people.

USING DATA TO TRACK PROGRESS

Community college leaders are responsible for the acquisition and incorporation of data to provide a quantitative and qualitative analysis for implementation and progress evaluation. In addition to direct observation, a measurable system must be in place with appropriate metrics to provide immediate feedback. It is important to be clear on which quantifiable metrics, or key performance indicators (KPIs), will be used to provide immediate information about the progress of the initiative—whether it's on or off plan.

In determining what metrics will be used, it is important to remember that quantity is not a proxy for quality. Optimally, the metrics will be obvious components of a well-defined project plan, representing clear institutional goals. The use of this information, and its analysis, can inform the leader's decision making, and also serve as an early warning indicator for a failing project.

Davila, Epstein, and Shelton suggest that monitoring performance is only part of the work of an innovation measurement system. They believe that measurement systems, if well used, should do more. They should serve as managerial facilitators, aiding the organizational leader in optimizing the implementation of a change initiative. This more dynamic system should fulfill three specific duties:

1. Plan: A measurement system that captures the logic behind an innovation strategy and facilitates agreement in terms of what is important, how day-to-day activities add value, and how each person contributes to the mission.
2. Monitor: When used to monitor implementation, the measurement system can identify deviations from the plan that require managerial action. In this context, a measurement system is used by exception (thus liberating managers' attention from constant supervision of the process) instead of as a way to stimulate discussion or to make a business model explicit.
3. Learn: Facilitation of ongoing discussion with an organization will lead to better innovation and execution. This involves learning about new solutions to achieving performance goals, as well as new business or technology options.[30]

The authors' proposed expanded role of innovation measurement provides an opportunity for leaders to see beyond simple monitoring to a more comprehensive methodology as they determine the efficacy of change and innovation.

The data and monitoring systems used for reporting innovation progress need not be overly complex. Ideally they would be tied into a college's existing ERP (Enterprise Resource Planning) or data management system. To the degree that the institutional research office can be involved in the process of metric creation and data tracking, further credibility is brought to the work and the reported progress.

In many cases, the preferred quality tool for monitoring is a dashboard. However, scorecards, depending on design, can also facilitate the management of organizational performance and provide a basis of comparison to industry benchmarks. The advantage of a dashboard is that it measures an organization's performance of particular initiatives. Both are often software-based tools that effectively transmute change and innovation strategy into a visual account of progress toward set targets.

A particularly impressive dashboard used by Grand Rapids Community College (GRCC) in Michigan is keyed to three particular areas of board focus: Student Success Pathways, Workforce Pathways, and Transfer Pathways. The model is elegant in simplicity, yet allows a focus for the institution and evaluates progress with seventeen indicators. Since this is a multiyear effort, the dashboard also includes comparisons from the previous year and a visual cue to overall trends. The dashboard is reviewed regularly by the college's leadership and trustees, and it is shared with employees so that they likewise remain focused on organizational priorities.

ERRORS AND ADJUSTING THE INNOVATION
INITIATIVE ON THE FLY

In the course of advancing change and innovation, a leader will encounter variables or deviations that may or may not have been anticipated. These factors may be directly observed by the leader or another, or made clear by monitoring system metrics. Regardless of the origin of the alert, it is the responsibility of the organizational leader to determine the magnitude of the problem and evaluate whether the original goals of the initiative can still be accomplished, and, if not what other options might be available.

In the course of leadership, there will always be occasions when, despite your best efforts, unexpected problems emerge. That's not failure per se, it's just life. Still, as the leader, you must be able to quickly adapt to the challenges before you. Such was the case on one particular day on the sailboat when my wife and I encountered an unanticipated, thick, lingering, and dangerous fog. I had a choice at the time: return to my home port or press on.

Guiding my decision making were the following key points: I was a little more than halfway through the voyage, so it was a toss-up regarding direction. It was still daytime—even though I could not see the sun through the fog, it nonetheless provided higher levels of illumination than at night, which was helpful. Finally, we had the essential safety equipment aboard and a full tank of fuel.

I opted to press on to the next harbor. This was a judgment call based upon available evidence, confidence, and an overall assessment of risk. That said, we made a series of tactical adjustments as well. I moved the ship closer to shore, hoping to capture some heat radiation from the shoreline. I slowed the engine. I audibly signaled our location regularly. My wife went to the bow of the boat to serve as an extension of my sight. I increased the boat's external illumination, and I studied the radar as we continued. Though we made it to the new port, it was a risk. Our voyage could have ended in a collision with another boat or worse.

The same basic principles hold true for organizational leaders regarding innovation. There will always be inherent risks when change is undertaken (though hopefully not risks to life and limb). Failure is always a distinct possibility. It is part of the process and, frankly, it's the price of admission into this work. But failure can also lead to positive outcomes, as was the case for 3M and Post-It notes. Mistakes are, in some ways, an important part of the process.

As the leader of your organization, when you are faced with an error, oversight, or just an outright mistake, how you choose to react to it will not only define you and your leadership but it will also have a lasting effect upon those whom you lead. The crew wants to see a confident captain at the helm when the seas are high, the foredeck is awash with waves, the wind is howling, and the boat is being pitched about. They also want to be actively involved in problem-solving.

POST-HOC EVALUATION

Having now moved through the entire process of innovation, and successfully, or possibly unsuccessfully, and having implemented all four of the SAIL battens, one final step remains—informing the future. By virtue of having implemented a change or innovation, all participants have gained experience, the prompt documentation of which will be helpful the next time around. Intentionally collecting the experiences of others involved, evaluating the ideas, discussing them, debating them, and considering what you would have done with the benefit of hindsight are part of the quality process.

One of the total quality process elements that I find helpful is quite simple—it's called Plus/Delta. At the end of most meetings at Jackson College, we ask all participants to tell us what worked well for the meeting (i.e., Plus) and, conversely, to share with us things that could have been improved upon (i.e., Delta). A similar "closing-the-loop" process was popularized by total quality management guru W. Edwards Deming, who created the Plan-Do-Check-Act (PDCA) model as a way for moving through a process, ultimately learning from past action in order to improve upon future action.[31]

The post-hoc evaluation can also provide a valuable historical record that can be used by others who may be interested in replicating and/or continuing your work. This applies particularly to lengthy change initiatives, such as cultural adjustments, that may carry on into the future. Thoughtful, summative discussion is central to learning organizations and supports transformation, adaptation, and change. Remaining disciplined about the post-hoc evaluation process is a habit that will pay dividends in the long term.

NOTES

1. Mark Eaton, "Why Change Programmes Fail." *Training Journal* (February 2010): 53–57. Accessed on April 3, 2014. http://search.proquest.com.proxy.lib.umich.edu/docview/202957937/fulltext/2B1942C43BE04818PQ/2?accountid=14667.

2. Sidharth Thakur, "Gleicher's Formula: A Scientific Approach to Change." Troy, NY: Bright Hub Project Management (2011). Accessed December 6, 2014. http://www.brighthubpm.com/change-management/122241-gleichers-formula-a-scientific-approach-to-change/.

3. Anne Kress, personal communication to author, December 5, 2014.

4. Ibid.

5. Keely Wilson and Yves L. Doz, "10 Rules for Managing Global Innovation," *Harvard Business Review* (October 2012): 84–90.

6. Paul Shoemaker and Steven Krupp, "The Power of Asking Pivotal Questions." *MIT Sloan Management Review* 56 (Winter 2015): 39–47.

7. Ibid., 40.

8. Ellen Langer, *Mindfulness: 25th Anniversary Edition* (Boston, MA: Da Capo Press), 2014.

9. Ellen Langer, "Mindfulness in the Age of Complexity." *Harvard Business Review* (March 2014): 68–73.

10. Ibid.

11. Ibid.

12. Ibid., 70.

13. Tony Davila, Marc J. Epstein, and Robert D. Shelton. *Making Innovation Work: How to Manage It, Measure It, and Profit from It* (Upper Saddle River, NJ: Pearson Education, 2006), 119.

14. Gary P. Pisano, "You Need an Innovation Strategy: It's The Only Way to Make Sound Trade-Off Decisions and Choose the Right Practices." *Harvard Business Review* (June 2015): 48–50.

15. Jeff Marsee, "10 Steps for Implementing Change." *NACUBO Business Officer* (June 2002): 36–41.

16. Ibid.

17. As quoted in Bryan Setser and Holly Morris, "Building a Culture of Innovation in Higher Education: Design & Practice for Leaders." *Educause*. Accessed on May 31, 2015. www.2revolutions.net/CultureofInnovation_HigherEd_4.15.15_FINAL.pdf.

18. Ibid., 33.

19. David B. Yoffie and Michael A. Cusumano, *Strategy Rules: Five Timeless Lessons from Bill Gates, Andy Grove, and Steve Jobs* (New York: HaperCollins, Publishers, 2015), 79.

20. Complete College America, "Remediation: Higher Education's Bridge to No-where." Washington DC, *Complete College America*. Indianapolis, Indiana: Author, 2012. Accessed January 5, 2014. http://www.completecollege.org/docs/CCA-Remediation-final.pdf.

21. Ibid.

22. Ibid.

23. As quoted in Tyler Hamilton, "Crisis Reset Economy: Immelt. GE Chief Says Investing in Innovation in 'Worst of Times' Will Sharpen Firms' Competitive Edge." Thestar.com. Tech News 11 (February 2009). Accessed on March 3, 2014. http://www.thestar.com/business/tech_news/2009/02/11/crisis_reset_economy_immelt.html.

24. Kaplan, *The Business Model Innovation Factory: How to Stay Relevant When the World is Changing*, xix.

25. Marsee, "10 Steps for Implementing Change," 39.

26. Jeffery M. Hiatt and Timothy J. Creasy, *Change Management: The People Side of Change* (Loveland, Co: Proci, Inc., 2012).

27. Kress, personal communication to author, December 5, 2014.

28. Ibid.

29. Hiatt and Creasy, *Change Management: The People Side of Change*, 9.

30. Tony Davila, Marc J. Epstein, and Robert D. Shelton, *Making Innovation Work: How to Manage It, Measure It, and Profit From It* (Upper Saddle River, NJ: Pearson Education, Inc., 2006), 148–49.

31. W. Edwards Deming, *Out of the Crisis* (Cambridge, MA: MIT Press, 1986).

Afterword

Forward, Ever Forward

"Innovation has nothing to do with how many R&D dollars you have. When Apple came up with the Mac, IBM was spending at least 100 times more on R&D. It's not about money. It's about the people you have, how you're led, and how much you get it."
—Steve Jobs

Forward, ever forward. I chose these words because I believe that community college leadership in the new economy cannot be about looking back, missing things of the past. To the extent that we are regularly looking over our shoulder, we become unfocused on the present, and we fail to contemplate and prepare for what is yet to come.

Still, we do have a responsibility to the lessons of the past, using those experiences and knowledge to inform and guide us on our journey forward. Whatever the future brings, it will most assuredly require a stubbornness and a resolute will from those in leadership roles to seize and, to the extent possible, to create the best possible future for their college.

PAYING ATTENTION

Going forward, community college leaders should be about paying attention to the present and the future, opportunities and threats, changing market dynamics, and, most importantly, to the people who make innovation possible. Leaders translate these observations into actionable responsibilities for themselves, for others in their organizations, for students, and for communities. Ideally, they also cultivate an adaptive organizational culture.

This is a sea change, a time of rapid, opaque, unpredictable, and sometimes involuntary change. Leaders need to watch the metaphorical sails and observe the water, constantly evaluating the business model to avoid becoming "Netflixed" and, more importantly, preparing to ensure relevance for the future. Some organizational leaders may tell you that their organizational success was the result of their excellent planning, distinctive insights, and solid strategy.

While that may be true on occasion, few people are that good. It is more likely that success also involves a fair degree of luck, a culture of

145

innovation, capable staff, and a willingness to risk in a very dynamic, competitive, global environment.

If you want to know the real story about the practical realities of undertaking change and innovation, talk to those leaders who exhibit humility, who seek meaning in their work, who are keen observers (constantly looking to the horizon), who ask questions, who pursue opportunity, and those who routinely rethink the way they do business, continuously looking to improve. You won't get any fish stories from them.

ORGANIZATIONAL PIVOTING

For some community colleges, the advancement of organizational change, and particularly the cultural development needed as a competitive deterrent, will be less an overhaul, and more a pivot, a moderate redirection of sorts. The global conglomerate General Electric, for example, founded in 1892 by Thomas Alva Edison, is recognized as one of the world's most revered innovators.

In 2013, GE CEO Jeffrey Immelt and his executive team concluded that it was necessary to pivot the company away from the majority of its consumer finance division, GE Capital, which it had productively operated for many years, and, instead, refocus its energies on the company's founding principles of innovation and manufacturing in new ways. The intentions of this inflection point were announced in 2015, and it was projected to take two years to complete.[1] In the words of the company's CFO Jeff Bornstein, "We had to decide whether we wanted to be a tech company that solves the world's big problems or a finance company that makes a few things."[2]

The "telltales" were indicating to Immelt that a relatively moribund stock price was problematic in the long term, and that changes in the emerging-market national economies posed significant opportunities for GE. For example, the McKinsey Global Institute's research indicated that by 2025, those national economies would be spending over $20 trillion per year on such infrastructure items as roads, water systems, airports and electrical grids, as well as myriad new consumer products that GE could lead the market in making.[3]

To help spur the redirection, and to reemerge as a strong innovator, the company is refocusing on the principles of its founder. For example, employees are now strongly encouraged to generate innovative ideas, which are vetted by a newly established "Growth Board." The Growth Board uses an entrepreneurial venture capital model to determine which ideas receive seed funding to spur experimentation and prototyping, and which ideas ultimately get a green light for production. The company expects that this new approach will reduce idea-to-production cycle time from years to a few months.

Uncharacteristically, GE is calling upon innovators outside of their organization by incorporating crowd sourcing methods to invite other entrepreneurs to review the company's challenges and submit their own proposals. As an incentive, GE provides cash distributions for ideas and "out-of-the-box" solutions to the company's thorniest problems.

One of the first crowd sourcing requests was for a 3-D printable jet engine bracket. The request drew nearly seven hundred entries from people in the global engineering community, representing fifty-six countries, with the winning entry coming from Indonesia. The result was a bracket that is 84 percent lighter than the original.[4] The solution was innovative, as was the manner by which the company went about addressing the problem.

Paying attention, whether to the economy, competition, technology, or founding principles, can prompt leaders to constantly question old assumptions and pivot the organization toward new ways of thinking, new ways of working, and perhaps even new business models to better position for the future.

RETHINKING OUR CURRENT MODEL

Another part of our responsibility as community college leaders is to constantly evaluate what currently *is*, in light of what could be. We have arrived at a point where the practicality of a comprehensive community college is inherently unsustainable on a go-forward basis. Emerging in its place are networked, competitive, beliefs-driven institutions that focus on niche and core areas of institutional competency.

The community college of the twenty-first century cannot weather the mile-wide, inch-deep service role of the past, as our stakeholders' elevated expectations won't permit it. Rather, and especially given the level of resource availability, we need to be honest with ourselves about what we can reasonably do, and do well. For those services and programs that we cannot effectively perform, we should either collaborate with other providers to achieve our mission objectives, or cease the effort altogether.

Not everything needs to be under our direct control in the new economy. Such considerations will require serious soul searching on the part of college leaders, leadership teams, and governing boards. We will be required to give mindful attention to the global community and the higher education landscape. Ultimately, we will need to make informed and purposeful choices based upon where we anticipate the industry to be heading.

The determination of which specific heading or pivot an organization should take is always a difficult task. On October 12, 2012, *The Chronicle of Higher Education* published a special report entitled "College, Reinvented." The article offered a thought-provoking list of ideas for re-creating higher education institutions in the face of societal change. Suggestions ranged from having two presidents for each college to remaking community colleges with a focus on the students they really serve, for example, those requiring developmental education, rather than the students they seek through recruitment practices.[5]

We can extract common themes from these and other suggestions, as well as from our own experience. Enrollment growth, the long-held metric of institutional success, is no longer a satisfactory proxy for institutional quality. Likewise, access, which may have been the right priority for the early community college, is an insufficient indicator of success given today's mandates.

Successful community colleges of the future will be champions for change, innovation, and quality. They will provide environments for experimentation, including failure. Their leaders will be able to differentiate fads and interesting notions from true, credible innovations. Successful colleges will adapt new business models and associated actions and measures that support new priorities—student success and completion.

Institutions that avoid the implications of this future view may survive, but as needs change, they will disappoint the communities and constituencies they were designed to serve. Over time, these institutions will struggle while their competitors, for example, for-profits, private nonprofits, and new entrants, gain market share. I believe that a continuing focus upon change, adaptation, innovation, and transformation must be hardwired into our methods, planning, and visioning as an institutional way of life.

For some leaders, a more palatable alternative to advancing innovation may be to allow peer institutions to slog through the challenges of innovation, to observe the effects from a distance, and to make changes at their own institutions only after the ideas have proven to be viable. These leaders may find reassurance in the fact that others are successful in implementing the innovation, thereby reducing the element of risk for their institution.

Indeed, this can be a sensible strategy and has been used effectively for years by many. Avoiding the high-risk proposition of being a first adopter of a particular innovation is an inherently safe strategy. In addition, some institutions may not have the resources to engage in a strong push toward innovation, so a more conservative approach may be their only option. Whether first-in or riding the wave, innovation is the only option for the future.

CHANGE AND INNOVATION AS A WAY OF INSTITUTIONAL LIFE

The macro-challenge of our time is to continuously ready the organization for change while appropriately responding to the deep-seated inclination of employees to keep things as they are. I find this challenge especially interesting when set against data collected from a national poll conducted by Right Management, which revealed that 83 percent of people currently employed in the United States are looking for another job because they are not feeling engaged.[6]

According to Scott Ahlstrand, Right Management's global practice leader for employee engagement, "High employee dissatisfaction has a ripple effect that can hurt the bottom line, disrupt productivity and damage morale. Successful companies cultivate and retain top talent by building loyalty through engagement that connects employees' work contributions to concrete business outcomes."[7]

I suspect that a fair share of employee dissatisfaction is driven by the pace of change and its attendant disruption. Employees may believe that the grass is greener on the other side of the fence where this is less change. However, that seems unlikely in the face of demographic, economic, and technology shifts that make stasis an untenable option for most industries.

Considering the statistics, community college leaders must do what they can to help employees prepare for change and cope with it through support, education, and ongoing communication. Trust with employees can be built and bolstered by sharing the message that you will be working through the change with them.

A related challenge facing organizational leaders is the fact that by the year 2025, as reported by *U.S. News & World Report*, 65 percent of the baby boomer generation will have moved into retirement. By 2030 every person in this generational category will be over 65 years of age and represent 20 percent of the population.[8]

These data points suggest that there is a tremendous change in the availability of talent on the horizon. Leaders should utilize this information to plan for the recruitment and retention of talent so that they are not caught short-handed. As suggested previously in this book, positioning the college for the effective recruitment and retention of new employees will be a great help to this end.

ARE WE ASKING THE RIGHT QUESTIONS?

The strategy of asking fresh questions when it comes to innovation is perhaps as much an art as it is a science. It is more creative than formulaic. Purposeful questioning can prompt new ideas and possibilities. We benefit from examining not only what we ask, but how we ask it, since doing so can reframe the problem for deeper consideration.

For example, rather than asking, How can we scale up this promising practice at our institution? we might consider instead, While this idea may work well in Pennsylvania, is it the right practice for our college or for our students? Instead of asking, Can we afford to build this new Health Education building? we might reframe the question as, What are the cost considerations for the expenditure of resources for this particular enterprise? Instead of asking, If we have to reduce the number of credit hours to complete a degree from sixty-five to sixty-two, how will students learn all they need to know to be successful? we might instead query, Given that degree completion credit hours must be reduced by three, what curricular adjustments must we make to ensure that the available course time provides the most essential information for students to be successful?

I suspect that as institutional leaders we don't do as effective a job as we could at listening to questions, or even forming them ourselves, because we are driven to move so quickly. Sometimes we remain fixed upon our own ideas, or we are emotionally tied to those ideas, and consequently we can see little else. We ask, What's the bottom line? for the sake of expediency rather than using questioning as an opportunity to observe, understand and create.

Consider also the use of even larger, more probing, future-scenario questions that provide unique insights to position the college. As one example, consider the current level of concern with financial aid and student loans. With well over $1 trillion in student loan debt—more than all the auto loans and credit card debt in the country—this is a significant national and institutional challenge.

Most of our organizations depend upon students' access to funding. Consider what colleges would do if conventional student loans were significantly reduced, more tightly controlled, or were returned to the financial industry for management? Discussions regarding the next reauthorization of the Higher Education Act (HEA) already suggest a need for "skin in the game" by higher education institutions, for example, partial repayment when students quit and default on taxpayer-subsidized student loans.

A related question regarding student loan default rates might be, How many times can community colleges go to the congressional well via HEA reauthorization or other legislation and ask for forbearance on penalties, making our case by citing student diversity, demographics, and the unique work that we do in community colleges?

While it is vital to ask thoughtful, probing, and complete questions, a president must also take care to ask questions of the right people. It is important to listen actively to people within the organization, not limiting our dialogue to the "usual suspects" who generally support our ideas. We must seek out other internal and external sources to gain the benefit of divergent opinions and thoughts.

This more inclusive approach affords college leaders the opportunity to broaden their perspective and break free from old paradigms. An intentional focus on people, both inside and outside the institution, can also help us to build understanding, reduce future mistakes, and, in general, model a process that may enable and empower others to ask their own questions and thereby contribute more fully to the innovation team.

WHAT'S AHEAD?

This book introduces the inflection point that is now before us. Insofar as our changed reality is increasingly marked by complexity, competition, and dynamism, our need for a course change is clear. We face an over-abundance of advice about how we should, and how others would, oper-ate our institutions. Consumer demand and technology are on the rise, and resources are on the decline. We have increasing numbers of stu-dents and other stakeholders who are expecting better results at a re-duced cost—that's a difficult formula for anyone to solve. Suffice to say, as I've noted throughout this book, innumerable, unavoidable forces are converging on higher education. The preponderance of evidence vali-dates the change mandate.

For community college leaders, it can be difficult to know how to best position our colleges, to decide which innovations to pursue, or where to place our limited resources. People are looking to us for the answers. Sometimes, as leaders, we may fall into the trap of thinking that we need to have all the answers—all the time. That's a false role image that we need to purge, and quickly.

There is no honor lost in ignorance, declaring that you need more time to further investigate, study, and evaluate a situation. Much like Langer proposes in her discussion about mindfulness, we have to find the space in our leadership roles to be comfortable not having all the answers. This acceptance is very different than idleness. Rather, we must remain open to the possibilities of change and innovation as we face future challenges in the service of others.

INNOVATIVE LEADERS

As part of the research for this book, I sought to uncover whether innova-tive community college leaders have similarities in approach, and wheth-er common skill sets aid their arrival at successful outcomes. I wanted to know if, at a personal level, there exists some key sociological or psycho-logical markers upon which success is predicated, something more mean-ingful than birth order, demographics, aptitude, attitude, family, or cul-ture. I wondered if there is something beyond the simple following of a series of rote steps to arrive at desired outcomes.

My findings from this exploration of leadership profiles were valuable on two levels. First, several paradoxes emerged. Within leaders' person-alities, successful CEOs were bold, but they valued organizational stability. They were visionary, yet practical. Risk-takers, yet cautious. Forceful and directive, yet collegial. They were empowered, yet they also empowered others to act.

I also discovered a consistent sense of personal strength, sometimes expressed as ego, which often masked profound humility—the kind of humility that comes from authenticity and from understanding that they are not all-knowing. Most of the community college leaders with whom I spoke readily admitted that they don't have all the answers, but they are trying to figure things out as best they can with the help of others.

Each spoke of an innate, deeply personal desire to help others—not expressed in the typical comments made for college catalogues or news stories, but at a very emotional, personal level. For them, this work is a calling of sorts. Each of them knew that this is where they are supposed to be, and this is the work that they are supposed to be doing.

These innovative presidents and other institutional leaders described to me the things that keep them awake at night, such as less-than-ideal student completion rates, insufficient funding to bring successful initiatives to scale, increasing levels of oversight and accountability, union contract negotiations, legislative intrusion, employee concerns, and virtually any issue that distracts them from helping students to be successful.

For some community college leaders, their worries had a name. Some presidents would mention a student who had a difficult upbringing and was now struggling to better himself or herself through education. Or they would offer the name of a student who didn't have the personal resources to continue college. Or they would recall the name of a student who overcame all odds to be there, only to have the college fail to get them across the finish line. It occurred to me that for most of these exemplary presidents and other leaders, the drive to improve their college has a name.

What I also witnessed in these leaders was a reflective, insightful, and deeply personal connection with, and investment in, the work of leadership. They seek to better themselves by investing in professional development and regular self-evaluation. They have abiding connections with peers, and they also have a solid life balance, taking time away to recharge.

Interestingly, they actively encourage employees to grow in their leadership as well, many serving to mentor or coach others professionally. Several established formal leadership development programs for employees at their college. Additionally, these leaders consistently try new things, and they are sometimes impatient to deploy change and innovation because they realize that delaying action can result in real students not walking across the stage to shake their hand at commencement.

NETFLIX POSTSCRIPT

One more thing about innovative organizations. Lest you think that any one innovator somehow has innovation all figured out, or has enough resources or experience to protect him or her from the competition, think again. Remember our earlier discussion of Blockbuster Video becoming "Netflixed?" On June 15, 2015 Beijing's Gehua CATV (cable TV) Network formally announced its plan to partner with e-commerce titan Alibaba, the National Radio and TV Network, and the China Film Company, China's largest producer and distributor of movies.

The new partnership intends to launch a movie streaming service and add thirty more major cable companies throughout China. If successful, the new company will be among the world's biggest and most influential film and TV companies, giving them significant sway in negotiating with any worldwide supplier of video entertainment.

Forbes magazine reported that this new development significantly jeopardizes the Los Gatos, California, firm, Netflix, which has been working intently to expand into international markets.[9] So even as leaders enjoy success by leapfrogging ahead to remain relevant, that success is still ephemeral. Thus the need to be watchful and to continuously innovate. That challenge is not limited just to business—it includes higher education as well.

A SMOOTH SEA NEVER MADE A SKILLFUL SAILOR

This book has also included bits of a personal and professional journey that led to the creation of a rather sensible, broad, and adaptable framework used to successfully advance change in organizations—the Strategy Archetype for Innovation and Leading (SAIL). To achieve organizational transformation, minimally, its four metaphorical battens (Leadership Preparation, Institutional Preparation, Assessment and Planning, and Execution and Evaluation) must be fully addressed within the organization, as research and practical experience have revealed.

As each batten is successfully completed, it provides the essential structure and the strength for the advancement of change and innovation, though success is never a guarantee. There are always those pesky, unanticipated factors that can emerge and potentially keep you from realizing your objective. Consequently, remaining alert to the winds of change, those unexpected externally-initiated changes (EICs), is a necessary skill for all leaders.

Much is unforeseen for sailors of the Great Lakes, but there are a few certainties, for example, the primacy of wind, maritime rules, communications protocols, and the like. The most fundamental truth, though, is that we have a limited sailing season in Michigan.

In January most folks begin eagerly to anticipate the coming season. In April they start preparing the boat and sails, installing new technology, and waiting for the moment of launch to arrive. In the lower Lake Michigan area, we splash our boat sometime in early May, if we are lucky. From spring to summer, if we make sailing a priority, we can have many amazing, joyful, and memorable experiences, learning as we go, and teaching others along the way. Then, after what seems like only a moment, the temperatures begin to drop, a sign of the coming fall season. In late October we pull the boat from the water, and the season is over, a memory.

Leadership at community colleges is, in some ways, like the sailing season. We must make the most of it while we're at the helm. Leadership is not easy. Indeed, it is often quite turbulent, choppy, and windy. Leadership does not take place on the glassy seas. Its full measure is made manifest in the rough sea conditions when we bring our best efforts to bear. At our colleges, we work hard to get the most out of our efforts in the service of others until the end of our work season, knowing that this work is a privilege. But until the season ends, we have an urgency to sail, and sail well.

So, as skipper of your boat, I offer you this advice. Make preparations, be vigilant in assessing the prevailing winds, monitor the sails and water, keep your eyes on the horizon, and care for your crew. If we want transformed institutions, we must pay mindful attention to the culture of our organization, help to adapt to a new and unfamiliar environment, and nurture it. We need to question, experiment, and learn. Inconsequential change (tweaks) and sustaining innovation alone will not transform our people, nor our organization.

We should invest in research and development and adopt new business models accordingly. We must create the right conditions and space for experimentation in our organizations. But most of all, we should be mindful that there is no single course or heading, no one right answer to the challenge of positioning our community colleges for the future. Indeed, being an innovator is both a blessing and a curse. But it is time to get going. Raise those sails, check the battens, and make your way to the deep water.

"He that will not sail till all dangers are over must never put to sea."
— Thomas Fuller

NOTES

1. Ted Mann and Victoria McGrane, "GE to Cash Out of Banking Business." *The Wall Street Journal*. Accessed on June 14, 2015. http://www.wsj.com/articles/ge-to-cash-out-of-banking-business-1428713151.

2. Rana Foroohar, "A Big Bet on Manufacturing: General Electric's Plan to Make Things Again is a Test for the Entire U.S. Economy." *Time* 20 (November 2014). Accessed December 1, 2014. http://time.com/3596974/ge-makes-a-big-bet-on-manufacturing/.

3. Ibid.

4. Steve Heller, "How the Community Helped General Electric Solve an Age-Old Problem." *The Motley Fool* 7 (December 2014). Accessed December 20, 2014. http://www.fool.com/investing/general/2014/07/13/how-the-community-helped-general-electric-company.aspx.

5. Scott Carlson, "College, Reinvented." *The Chronicle of Higher Education* 15 (October 2012). Accessed January 18, 2014. http://chronicle.com/article/College-Reinvented/135110/.

6. ManpowerGroup, "Most Employees Plan to Pursue New Job Opportunities in 2014, Reveals Right Management Poll." Accessed on June 27, 2015. http://www.prnewswire.com/news-releases/most-employees-plan-to-pursue-new-job-opportunities-in-2014-reveals-right-management-poll-232512501.html.

7. Ibid.

8. Tom Sightings, "5 New Realities of Retirement." Accessed on June 27, 2015. http://money.usnews.com/money/blogs/on-retirement/2014/12/02/5-new-realities-of-retirement.

9. Rob Cain, "Announcement of China's 'Netflix' May Be the Death Blow for Netflix in China." *Forbes*. Accessed June 16, 2015. http://www.forbes.com/sites/robcain/2015/06/16/announcement-of-chinas-netflix-may-be-the-death-blow-for-netflix-in-china/.

Index

About the Author

Dr. Daniel J. Phelan has served as president and CEO of Jackson College, located in Jackson, Michigan, since 2001. He serves at the pleasure of a seven-member Board of Trustees who are elected at-large for six-year terms. He holds a Ph.D. in higher education from Iowa State University in Ames, Iowa, and an M.B.A. from St. Ambrose University in Davenport, Iowa. He currently is chair-elect to the Board of Directors for the American Association of Community Colleges (AACC). He is also co-chair of AACC's Higher Education Act Reauthorization Task Force.

He served on the AACC's 21st-Century Commission on the Future of Community Colleges, co-chairing a team charged with redefining the community college role and mission. Dr. Phelan is past president of the Continuous Quality Improvement Network (CQIN) organization and past chair of the Michigan Community College Association (MCCA) Board of Directors. He is an active consultant-evaluator for the North Central Association of Colleges and Schools, Higher Learning Commission in Chicago, Illinois.

Dr. Phelan serves as a board member for the Center for Community College Student Engagement in Austin, Texas, and is a founding board member for the international organization, US-Brasil Connect. He is a member of the Jackson County Superintendent's Association, the Jackson County Enterprise Group, and the Lenawee Economic Development Corporation. He also serves as a board member for the Ronald McDonald House of Charities and as a member of the Board of Governors of the Jackson Area Chamber of Commerce. Dr. Phelan is married to Dr. Adriana Phelan. They have four daughters: Kathryn, Michelle, Maggie, and Isabella.